Raoul Sobel has been obsessed with Chaplin since his childhood, when his father kept him amused with fine Chaplin imitations and detailed descriptions of the plots of his films.

He works in the film and television industries, was at one time an editor in the B.B.C., but now directs, writes and edits a wide variety of films and television programmes from documentary to drama. He is also a free-lance writer and dramatist and a one-time member of the Royal Court Writers' Studio.

He currently lives in London.

David Francis has a life-long interest in the cinema. He joined the British Film Institute in 1959 as their first Television Acquisitions Officer and later became Deputy Curator of the National Film Archives. He also worked for B.B.C. television in charge of the World Cinema programme and bought American and Continental films for British audiences. It was while working on the restoration of Chaplin's short films for a B.B.C. season (Raoul Sobel was an editor on that project) that the idea for this book was first put forward.

David Francis is also interested in the pre-history of the cinema, and particularly in the magic lantern. He regularly presents magic lantern slides in Britain and on the Continent and has written articles and made a television programme on the subject.

He is now Curator of the National Film Archives at the B.F.I.

# Chaplin
## Genesis of a Clown

Raoul Sobel
and David Francis

QUARTET BOOKS
LONDON MELBOURNE NEW YORK

First published by Quartet Books Limited 1977
A member of the Namara Group
27 Goodge Street, London WIP IFD


Copyright © 1977 by Raoul Sobel and David Francis

Design by Jim Wire


Casebound ISBN 0 7043 2150 x
Paperback ISBN 0 7043 3134 9


Printed in Great Britain by The Anchor Press Ltd
and bound by Wm Brendon & Son Ltd
both of Tiptree, Essex

# Contents

# Acknowledgements

We would like to offer our appreciation to all those who have freely given encouragement, help and support, in particular the B.B.C. who unintentionally enabled us to examine Chaplin's early films in depth, the National Film Archive Stills Library and its enthusiastic staff who searched the depths of their collection for rare illustrations, Ellis Ashton, Chairman of the British Music Hall Society, who opened up to us his considerable collection of music hall memorabilia, the Cinema Bookshop and its mastermind Fred Zentner who loaned us some striking visual material, the Theatre Museum, at the Victoria and Albert, who gave us valuable information about the commedia dell' arte and Sylvia who typed the manuscript, corrected our spelling and punctuation, and suggested, sometimes forcefully, changes in the text.

# Foreword

In writing this book we have been guided by one overall consideration, to present Chaplin as a product of his time as well as an artistic phenomenon. Too often writers on the cinema tend to treat it as a spectacle conceived and executed in a vacuum, as if its creators were not subject to the same pressures, tastes, anxieties, hopes and needs as the mass audience they are trying to please. Unlike those who cater for a privileged few, film-makers have had to handle the raw material of the life surrounding them and in many cases to share it. By using an instrument whose peculiar distinction is being able to record that life disinterestedly they provide us, it could be argued, with much more of the flavour of an age than a painting or a play. Comedy, in particular, bears the stamp of its time, and Chaplin's achievement, though wholly inimitable, is largely derivative.

The films we have chosen to survey are from the beginning of 1914 to the end of 1917. This was the most prolific period of Chaplin's life, when he acted in sixty-three films and solely directed forty-one of them. Chaplin's screen characterization touched its greatest appeal and reached its fullest maturity in those years; most of the ideas that came after were extensions, embellishments, variations or pale reflections of the ones he explored then. By concentrating on the early films we hope to illuminate the core of his art and so provide a critical assessment that is applicable to all his work.

# Introduction

For nearly ten years, with the exception of one week which proved disastrous, the Crystal Hall cinema in New York played nothing but Chaplin films. It has been estimated that up till 1921, cinemas running Chaplin shorts reaped a wild harvest of $25 million.

As early as 1916, the *Tatler*, not known for being precipitate, felt constrained to say:

> Charlie's extraordinary success as a cinema actor has created a vogue that is as great as that achieved by many a more distinguished character in history such as the 'fat boy' in Pickwick, Bluebeard, Casabianca, Jumbo and Humpty-Dumpty. The lineaments of Mr Chaplin are known to the uttermost ends of the earth and his face may be described as one upon which the sun never sets.

The very fact that a reputable magazine like the *Tatler* could write about Chaplin reflected the widening split within the Chaplin myth – on one side the buffoon, on the other the serious thinker. Over the years Chaplin chose to cultivate the second role, advising a prime minister on how to solve his country's problems, expatiating on the dangers of the world monetary system or the hazards of capital punishment, dispensing thoughts on Art and Comedy, and generally calling a fair proportion of the European intelligentsia his 'good friends'. The 'Little Fellow's' mask was jettisoned once and for all when at the première of *Monsieur Verdoux* he turned to some children who were following him with cries of 'Charlie! Charlie!' and said, 'This is the new Charlie.' Perhaps when, in 1916, Minnie Maddern Fiske, the great American actress, used names like Aristophanes, Plautus, Shakespeare and Rabelais in an article eulogizing the tramp, she was unwittingly sowing the seeds of his dissolution.

The public he turned his back on, the original raw recruits to the cinema who habitually took their laughter straight without having to add a dash of culture to make it palatable, did not desert him. In September 1933, in *Woman's Home Companion*, he wrote about his visit to London two years previously:

They are my people, these Cockneys. I am one of them. As I look into their eyes I see that spiritual hunger, that inner craving. Their emotions have made them inarticulate. They are only expressed by the eager clutching of my sleeve. How little must come into their lives! How appreciative they are for the trivial thing that I've done.

The trivial thing he had done, of course, was to become the world's most highly paid and successful comedian, but behind the unctuousness of the words one can discern a simple fact: he was still held in overwhelming affection by the public to whom he no longer belonged. Even their children had inherited the myth, so that well into the 1930s they could still be heard singing, to the tune of 'Gentle Jesus':

'Charlie Chaplin, meek and mild,
Took a sausage from a child.
When the child began to cry,
Charlie slapped him in the eye.'

Yet from 1923 to the release of *Monsieur Verdoux* in 1947, the 'Little Fellow' had appeared in only five films, two of them, *Modern Times* and *The Great Dictator*, hardly representative of the wistful figure a world-wide audience had first come to love in the films made during the First World War. Some might argue that this proved Chaplin's creation to be timeless, that in spite of his changing style, indeed in spite of the whole evolution of the cinema, the image of the boots, bowler hat and cane lingered on like an unconscious, tribal memory. Without querying whether sixty years is a sufficient test of timelessness, it is possible to guess that the reasons for the 'Little Fellow's' persistence are much more complex than many of his most ardent supporters imagine.

# One

'We built the modern style movie industry on the star system, but the public made the stars. All the skill of the directors and all the booming of press-agent drums will not make a star. Only the audience can do it. Some quality of the player – often elusive – is translated by the screen to the audience' – Adolph Zukor, *The Public is Never Wrong* (1954)

When Chaplin arrived on the Keystone lot in 1913, the star system had been operating for just three years. 'System' is something of a misnomer. It was not a rational policy carefully thought out by producers with an eye to the public's needs. Since the industry had begun, they had done their utmost to suppress any sign of an actor being recognized by his name. Instead they insisted that all their players should shelter behind the company symbol in docile anonymity. Trade journals, posters, advertisements made no mention of a public favourite other than to remind the reader that he or she was a company product, so that Florence Lawrence was known as 'The Biograph Girl', and Florence Turner as 'The Vitagraph Girl'. When the *New*

Florence Lawrence – 'the Biograph Girl'

Florence Turner – 'the Vitagraph Girl'

*York Dramatic Mirror* received a letter from a reader innocently asking the name of a player in a Biograph film, 'Spectator' thundered back:

> The company holds, as The Spectator understands it, that it is not the personality of particular players that makes for success in picture production, and this without desiring to detract from the good work of the people who have appeared in Biograph films. The essential elements of successful film production are, the Biograph is believed to argue, first the story, second the direction, and third competent people as a class and not as individuals. These views are not far different from those advanced by The Spectator . . .

The reply was disingenuous. Anonymity was not due to any feeling for priorities in film-making, nor to any team spirit or incipient socialism on the part of the producers – simply that they wished to avoid the inconvenience of having to pay higher salaries. If a film were to be sold on the name of its leading actor, there was no telling how powerful a weapon it could become when discussing new contracts. There was also the very real fear of competition, which in the feverish days of the film pioneers bore a striking similarity to cattle rustling. Producers would not think twice about stealing an actor from another company with all the inducements they could offer, and then building up their own business on the strength of his popularity. When Florence Lawrence joined Carl Laemmle's company, he trumpeted throughout the trade journals that, 'The Biograph Girl is now an IMP.' When Augustus Carney, with the unlikely screen name of 'Alkali Ike', changed horses, as it were, and joined Broncho Billy, he became 'Universal Ike'.

Some of the lengths the producers went to in guarding their stables were enormous. Biograph had a particularly bad record in this respect, not allowing any details of production, technicians, writers or directors to leave the studio. D. W. Griffith, himself unknown to his admirers, refused to allow Mary Pickford to read her fan mail in case her ideas rose above her station. *Motion Picture*'s 'Answer Man' was led to remark that 'there is a legend to the effect that Biograph players have their names locked in a big safe and only get them back when they leave the company'.[2]

However, the producers were not entirely to blame. Many actors preferred to bask in anonymity. The cinema was still not respectable, and to have one's name thrust on a screen in some such house of shame as a converted billiard saloon, or even a hick vaudeville theatre, was not good publicity for any player still aspiring to fame in the legitimate theatre. Even after the cinema had at last begun to make inroads into the realms of middle-class sensibility, trade journals could still report that, 'While the pictures have attained a distinct prominence and are now recognized as a standard attraction, the people playing in them are very sensitive about having their identity become known. They have an impression that the step from regular stage productions to the scenes before the camera is a backward one.'

The strange thing was that the theatre itself, except in very few instances, could hardly offer them a striking alternative. With the emphasis on more realism, the playwright and producer reigned supreme, and the days when big stars could demand a play built solely around their talents were passing.

Will the survival of the crop of modern playwrights compensate for the obsoletion of what for centuries has been the vital force of the stage? [bewailed a critic, in 1910.] Will the oblivion to which has been cast all but the memories of great individual figures reveal instead a perfect ensemble playing? . . . One cannot prophesy at this time what is to become of the immortal works of the greatest writers of all time, if there be no interpreters of the tremendous chief roles which all of their masterpieces contain.[3]

But tremendous roles, so to speak, had already infiltrated the cinema. Those intrepid foreigners, the French, much admired in the United States for their technical virtuosity, had produced in 1908 a film destined to lead a large part of the film industry into a blind alley from which it would not emerge until ten years later. *L'Assassinat du Duc de Guise* was deliberately launched to carry the cinema into the regions of pure art. Thenceforth any film which employed a stage cast, 'classical' material, and in which 'the figures are all of heroic size', as the *New York Dramatic Mirror* rather ominously put it, was to become known respectfully as 'Le Film d'Art'. Traces of its influence can still be found in those panoramic Hollywood productions which are immediately recognizable as being of serious import by dint of the actors moving and speaking at half their normal speed. Lafitte Brothers, who produced the *Duc de Guise*, left no doubt as to their intentions or their ultimate audience. All the players were from the Comédie Française, the script was written by an unimpeachable member of the Académie Française and the music was provided by no less a composer than Saint-Saëns. Charles Pathé, it was reported, had been moved to 'tears of admiration and homage' when he viewed it for the first time.

Its impact on the American critics was no less considerable. The *New York Dramatic Mirror* was moved to declare that 'its superior quality in photographic excellence, superb acting, rich settings and

In 1908, Film d'Art produced *L'Assassinat du Duc de Guise*, the first of a series of films based on stage plays and featuring actors from the theatre. Every scene was shot in one take from the same camera position

costumes and skilful dramatic handling of a carefully constructed picture narrative distinguishes it as one of the few masterpieces of motion picture production'.[4] It would obviously not elicit the same response today, but in defence of 'Le Film d'Art' one is bound to say that the classical tradition of acting made no pretence at realism but was a stylized, non-naturalistic language by which the actor had to communicate real emotion – something akin, one imagines, to classical ballet

The immediate effect on the film world, unfortunately, was to drive producers closer to the theatre. Not that they needed much encouragement. Vitagraph had lifted *Raffles* from the stage in 1905 for their first story film, and there was abounding evidence of other productions also based on stage successes, although unacknowledged. 'When you are sometimes required to turn out three scenarios during a single day, it is a great help to have standard literature to draw on,' says Wagenknecht in his delightful book *The Movies in the Age of Innocence*,[5] and he cites *As You Like It*, *Evangeline*, *Hiawatha*, *The Scarlet Letter* as masquerading in clothes borrowed from Kalem's wardrobe, and *The Squaw Man* as transmuted by Vitagraph into *Twixt Love and Duty*. This might not have been such a bad thing; after all, an original screenplay is the exception rather than the rule even today, but in those days to make a stage play into a film meant nothing

Production still showing the Jesse L. Lasky Feature Film Company on location in 1914 for Cecil B. De Mille's first film as a director, *The Squaw Man*

more nor less than to transport it intact to a film studio. The only change made was to shorten it. Thus when Mounet-Sully, a great French actor, made *Oedipus*, he refused to walk in front of the camera until every detail of the studio set matched every detail of the stage set. When this had been done, he insisted that he be photographed speaking every line of every important speech. The final film showed a series of voiceless monologues.

Fidelity to a stage set or slavish imitation of theatrical acting were not the only dangers. Far worse was the total disregard of any of the dearly bought advances that men like Griffith had already introduced into picture making – techniques like quick cuts or inter-cutting, using the camera at different heights, or the dramatic close-up. Most of the industry, it is true, was still hidebound by stage traditions, with the action confined within the proscenium frame and the camera limited to one point of view like the captive audience in a theatre. But 'Le Film d'Art' did nothing to hurry the process of change and most probably held it back.

This state of affairs, which might have led to hardening of the arteries in an industry only a few years old, was luckily being undermined by some of the people it most concerned: the film actors, the ones who had begun to understand the needs of the camera and to feel their own power at the box office. When in 1909 a relaxed, friendly man, whom millions were later to know as 'The Dimpled Darling', stood on the Vitagraph set and said simply, 'I am an actor and will not build sets or paint scenery,' he was not merely breaking with the unwritten law that said actors must make do as carpenters, scene-shifters, costume repairers and set-painters when not actually acting; by asserting his own status, Maurice Costello had set a movement in motion which eventually led to the film artist triumphing over his theatrical counterpart.

Vitagraph, the first company to defy the Motion Picture Patents Company, made Maurice Costello into one of the screen's first leading men

The second blow was struck when 'The Biograph Girl' suddenly vanished. The St Louis newspapers, without any apparent authority, published a story that she had been killed by a streetcar. Immediately Carl Laemmle, her new boss, spread advertisements everywhere stating that she was very much alive and his most recent acquisition. And that was not all. To prove it conclusively he announced that Miss Lawrence would be making a personal appearance to the myriads of her fans who still had no idea of her real name. When the train draw into St Louis, more people were there waiting for her than had been present the week before to welcome President Taft on an official visit. At last she was not just a well-known face, but also a name that could find its way into an autograph book or reach the giddy heights of an illuminated sign.

But there was still a long way to go. Producers were still besotted with the image of a big star in a big stage success who would lead the way to instant riches. Their life's dream must have seemed answered when, in 1912, Sarah Bernhardt, then aged sixty-eight, arrived in

Sarah Bernhardt was sixty-seven when, in 1911, she played the lead in *La Dame aux Camélias*, the film version of Alexandre Dumas's social drama.

Sarah Bernhardt made *Queen Elizabeth* in 1912, and Adolph Zukor bought it for American distribution. It was a commercial success and led to a spate of historical dramas featuring famous stage actors

America – on the silver screen. She appeared in *La Dame aux Camélias* and *Queen Elizabeth,* the one a favourite in popular literature and the other a thriving success on the Paris stage. From then onwards the cinema became a place sanctified for 'members of the profession'. It may be added in passing that Bernhardt had already appeared in vaudeville at a fee of $100,000 for twenty weeks' work, even though vaudeville had no better claim to respectability than the cinema.

Of the two films it was *Queen Elizabeth* that really brought in the much-hoped-for producer's bonanza. Bought for $18,000 by a Hungarian émigré named Adolph Zukor who had once been in the fur trade, it was presented on Broadway in 1912 by him and his partner, Daniel Frohman, who came from a very respected theatrical family. It achieved two positive results for the future of the industry: it vindicated feature-length films and its subject captured the middle-class attention so earnestly sought by the largely uneducated cinema businessmen. On the strength of it, Zukor formed his own company based on the slogan 'Famous Players in Famous Plays' and sent *Queen Elizabeth* on a countrywide progress from which she returned with a purse of $60,000.

The response from the stage actors was immediate. 'It rained stars like hailstones,' said William S. Hart, 'and like hailstones, they melted under the California sun.' As each player joined the movies the newspapers charted their course like falling meteorites, giving most attention to the salaries. These were ludicrously misleading. Based on the actor's eminence in the theatre world, they bore no relationship to his real worth in the cinema and served only to heighten the tension between the stage import and his seasoned rival in films. Thus we find the anomalous situation of Beerbohm Tree, then well past his prime, commanding $3,500 a week, Douglas Fairbanks, who had collected modest success on the stage, earning $200, and William S. Hart, a brilliant leading man who was a relative failure in the theatre, drawing a shameful $125.

Not that the truant stage artistes went unscathed. The old guard of critics reared up with fiery nostrils, one of them, Walter Pritchard Eaton, contending that failure on film should be seen as an accolade, conferring on an actor the undeniable proof of his talent. With incredible blindness he went on to say that only the worst actors, the 'hams', went on to make a successful career in films. To this criticism the actors made elevated replies, full of ghostly echoes of late-nineteenth-century romanticism. Bernhardt: 'I rely upon these films to make me immortal.' James K. Hackett: 'There is no death!' Sir Herbert Beerbohm Tree: 'The actor has hitherto lived for his generation. The cinema has given him the enfranchisement of posterity.'

W. G. Barker brought Sir Herbert
Beerbohm Tree, his entire cast,
costumes and scenery, from His
Majesty's Theatre to Ealing to film
five scenes of his stage success,
*Henry VIII*

Slowly but surely, however, the screen actors began to hold their own. Stars like John Bunny made series of pictures bearing their names, Bunny's including such gems as *Bunny's Birthday*, *Bunny in Disguise*, *Bunny Dips into Society*, until as Wagenknecht records, 'by 1913 the New Empire Theater in Detroit was setting up in electric lights "TODAY John Bunny & Flora Finch"'[6] without bothering to mention the name of the film. This was not surprising. What possible meaning could names like Bernhardt and Rejane and Beerbohm Tree and Mrs Fiske have had for the population of, say, Oshkosh, Nebraska? But John Bunny and Flora Finch were there with them, every week. And the early film audiences were realists. There was simply no use in explaining to them that Vitagraph had procured, at great expense, the distinguished services of Rose Coghlan to play Rosalind in *As You Like It*. All that they saw was a sixty-two-year old woman attempting a part for a girl a third of her age. In June 1912 and again in October 1913 the *Motion Picture Story Magazine* announced the winners of its popularity contest among the stars. On neither occasion was a great stage actor among them.

Meanwhile the stage fraternity were not exactly making their own future in films a secure one. They approached their new experiment with scepticism and condescension, arguing with directors and frequently causing fist-fights. 'If anyone could have seen us who had known His Majesty's!' sighed Constance Collier. 'I used to think of the scarlet-coated flunkeys with their white wigs, and the pomp and splendour of the theatre.'[7] Great days, perhaps, but wiser to remain tactful and not harp on them rather than irritate a film actor so much that he refuses to appear opposite you.

Oliver Morosco Film

THE CODE *of* MARCIA GRAY

*Featuring*
CONSTANCE COLLIER

The theatrical tradition was still strong when Constance Collier appeared in *The Code of Marcia Gray* in the United States in 1916

In fact, the film actors had only to stand back and watch while the stage stars ensured their own failure. Except for a notable few – among them George Arliss, Lionel and John Barrymore, Marie Dressler – they floundered helplessly. The new industry was alien to their temperament, training and experience. There was no audience to inspire them; the long waits between shooting were an affront to their status; the system of brief scenes photographed out of sequence ruined their concentration and made it almost impossible for them to sustain a mood or tempo; they could not stride about as on a stage for fear of going out of the camera's range; sudden movements or violent action were forbidden them; film lighting aged them; and most exasperating of all, they were at the mercy of a director and a barrage of technical paraphernalia which took the responsibility for their performance out of their own hands. The humiliation of acting opposite others who had never been to the great drama schools of Europe, but who had graduated from vaudeville or the circus, was bad enough, but the despair on seeing them stealing each scene with apparent ease must have been almost too great for the stage actors to bear. Had they been able to use their voices, they might have salvaged their reputation, but even this was denied them. A trick that was played on Sir Herbert Beerbohm Tree sums up the difference between the two worlds:

Sir Herbert did not understand the method of picture-making, and had long arguments with the director as to whether the whole text of Shakespeare should be spoken or not. He won, as ever, and insisted on speaking every word. But the cameraman was obstinate too. He invented a dummy machine, and kept the two cameras working at the same time. The dummy didn't register anything, but satisfied Sir Herbert, and when the speeches came to an end the real camera took the picture.[8]

It is to Sir Herbert's credit that when he found out he laughed.

At last, with the names of Chaplin, Mary Pickford, Douglas Fairbanks, Arbuckle, and a host of others drumming on the door, the producers had to let reality in. Money was being lost on the stage stars and amassed on the rest. In 1918, the box office returns forced into the open a fact that everyone had known for a long time. *Current Opinion* wrote: 'The giants of the stage are pygmies artistically on the screen.'[9] And Jesse Lasky, of the Jesse J. Lasky Feature Film Company, who had filmed the huge stage success *The Squaw Man* and had run neck-and-neck with Zukor in presenting theatre names before unimpressed film audiences, could glumly admit that, 'Our experiment has not been a great success. We have found that the screen can borrow very little from the stage.' The battle was over. Screen actors, and with them the star system, had triumphed.

*1. References*

1. *New York Dramatic Mirror*, 16 July 1910.
2. *Motion Picture*. Quoted by E. Wagenknecht, *The Movies in the Age of Innocence*, University of Oklahoma Press, 1962
3. Robert Grau, *The Business Man in the Amusement World: a Volume of Progress in the Field of Theater*, New York: Broadway Publishing Company, 1910.
4. *New York Dramatic Mirror*, 27 February 1909.
5. E. Wagenknecht, *The Movies in the Age of Innocence*, op. cit.
6. ibid.
7. Constance Collier, *Harlequinade*, London: John Lane, 1929.
8. ibid.
9. *Current Opinion*, quoted in George C. Pratt, *Spellbound in Darkness*, New York: University School of Liberal and Applied Studies, University of Rochester, 1966.

# Two

'He is, I believe, the most widely known man in the world. They know him almost as well in Japan and Paraguay and Spain as we do here. Because of that he has attained an almost legendary significance in the eyes of millions of people; they give him something akin to the homage given to Bernhardt and Shakespeare and John L. Sullivan. These millions could never have that feeling for a Senator, a diplomatist, a millionaire. But Charlie! "What is he like?" they say, breathlessly. "How does he walk and talk?" ' – Harvey Higgins in *New Republic* (3 February 1917)

Apart from those who had hired him, Chaplin was unknown in the film world. Even more pertinent, as far as the star system was concerned, there was nothing to sell, for the 'Little Fellow' had yet to be created. He was nearly twenty-five, acted much older, was evidently shy and certainly difficult. His reception at first was frosty, Mabel Normand, Keystone's leading comedienne, calling him 'that Englisher so-and-so', but gradually the ice thawed as admiration for his talent grew. What is not so clear is whether that admiartion carried with it genuine liking for the man. And that takes us to the heart of the major quandary about Chaplin. Can the feelings of love, warmth, sadness, mirth and nostalgia which the 'Little Fellow' evoked be entirely misplaced if extended towards its creator?

The artist's achievement is plain, though a sea of academic ink has all but submerged it. His character on, the other hand, is far from plain, and made even less so by conflicting opinions. These range from public condemnation as a licentious subversive, to outright adoration as a seer for the suffering masses. Private comments are almost as contradictory, and accounts of his life differ on some of the most basic things like dates and places. More often than not it is difficult to determine whether his detractors or devotees are talking about the 'Little Fellow', the technician, the artist or the man himself. Inevitably one is led to the conclusion that Chaplin does not exist, or, at least, that a cohesive unity known as 'Chaplin' never appears fully at any one time. It could be held that this applies to all of us, that no one is the same at seven o'clock in the morning as at seven o'clock at night. But there is an essence, a chart as it were, called Mr A or Mr B on which various lines of mood, health, thoughts, activity and so on can be drawn. In Chaplin's case it is not the pattern of the lines that changes, but the chart itself. The most obvious explanation is that he himself does not know what the chart is, that the long hours of introspection which he indulged in throughout his life bore no real fruit but were fantasies on a theme which was itself a fantasy. In other words, to come to a knowledge of oneself one has to organize a relationship with an outside world; but if that world is part of one's own imaginings, then self-quest takes on the image of a never-ending corridor of mirrors. Thomas Burke, in the most perceptive essay there is on Chaplin the man, puts it like this:

> He is first and last an actor, possessed by this, that or the other. He lives only in a role, and without it he is lost. As he cannot find the inner Chaplin, there is nothing for him, at grievous moments, to retire into; he is compelled to merge himself, or be merged, in an imagined and superimposed life. He can be anything you expect him to be and anything you don't expect him to be, and he can maintain the role for weeks. If he likes you he will be what you expect him to be. If he has one of his perverse moods, he will be something that jars.[1]

In view of what Burke says, it would seem a pretty futile task to search for the real Charlie in and out of the opinions that litter his career. At best one can take cognizance of the things they agree on, as, for example, his amazing gift for mimicry, his dislike of alcohol, his attraction to women much younger than himself, his moodiness, his hatred of war (as against violence which crops up in all his films) and his basic loneliness. Unfortunately his autobiography, which arrived in 1964, is more interesting for the manner of its telling than for the tale. Though the description of his early life makes interesting reading, there is no mention of some of the people who had the greatest influence on his career, and most of the rest is a catalogue of great names who paid him fashionable obeisance or who swept through his life dropping maxims like sugared plums. It does little justice to either the man or the artist, and one can understand Kenneth Tynan's disappointment on reading it as someone who had idolized Chaplin for years.[2] The last word on it should be given, perhaps, to a man who knew and worked with him for thirty-six years, his personal cameraman, Roland Totheroh, who is not given a mention in the book but is one of the few reliable commentators on Chaplin's working methods and personality.

Roland H. ('Rollie') Totheroh began
his association with Chaplin in 1915,
and it continued until his retirement
in 1954. Here he is seen preparing to
photograph a scene from *Sunnyside*
in 1919.

A lot of Charlie's autobiography to me is false, because I knew
him so well. He's building himself up for a pinnacle I don't think he
ever reached. As a genius, yes; he *is* a genius. He can talk on pretty
near any subject. But if a person really was educated on the subject
he was talking on, they'd see the errors that he made. He always
figured his masses, his public, no matter what he does. 'Oh, they'll
think it's great.'[3]

What, then, is left? The past, it seems. Though Chaplin's talent
may well be timeless, the man was a product of his time, and it is
almost uncanny how some of the pressures of late Victorian and
Edwardian London are very nearly reproduced in Chaplin's thoughts
and actions. Obviously one makes no claim that all is suddenly re-

vealed, but as a rough measure of the man it seems to bear out Lamartine's claim that, 'History is neither more nor less than biography on a large scale.'

## 2. References

1. Thomas Burke, *City of Encounters*, London: Constable, 1932.
2. Kenneth Tynan in the *Observer*.
3. R. E. Totheroh in *Film Culture*, Spring 1972.

# Three

'None of us can move beyond the point of our awakening. We may range about it, but if we try to get way from it, we find we are tethered to it; and if Charles today is hard and cold, it is because his first decade was hard and cold – orphanage, back streets, back rooms, broken boots, fish and chips; the craven ugliness of poverty and the mordant strain of it' – Thomas Burke, *City of Encounters* (1932)

There is probably no other age in English history which has caused so much controversy as the Victorian age. Its documentation is immense: a plethora of government commissions and findings, tracts by committed dreamers or activists, horrified prognostications by philosophers, secret memoirs from twilight walkers, lurid articles by professional journalists, appalling statistics from amateur reformers, Gothic novels, salon ballads, street songs and music-hall patter. Since the Victorians themselves quarrelled over the meaning of all this evidence, it is no wonder that twentieth-century scholars, picking their way through the bewildering undergrowth, should do exactly the same. The one consistent point of agreement, however, is that interpretation depends on direction. If a person steps out of a London hotel and walks in any direction he chooses he will end up with a completely different impression from the one he would have received had he taken the opposite route. Thus with the Victorian age. One traveller might find a cluster of enlightened Education Acts whereas another might find unpleasant figures on child mortality. Of course, the impression also depends on the class of traveller. 'Enlightened' might very well have sprung to the lips of a high-minded late Victorian, but to a working man, struggling to feed his family of, say, eight on a weekly diet in which the only protein is $2\frac{1}{2}$ ounces of fish on Sunday, the Education Acts could well have been an irrelevance. It is a question of viewpoint, and though the period from 1889, when Chaplin was born, to the death of Victoria in 1901 is generally considered to be a prosperous one, it is as well to bear in mind that at the beginning of our own century the Fabians brought out a series of pamphlets which proved that a third of the population of the richest country in the world lived 'in chronic poverty, unable to satisfy the primal needs of animal life'.[1]

That said, it is nevertheless true that, no matter to what degree, the prosperity managed to affect almost every level of society. Children growing up around the turn of the century could have travelled by tram, rail, the underground or motor-car, though the last two were more common towards the end of the period. Bicycling clubs were springing up all over the country as the population began to take an active interest in its environment. Bank holidays and days by the sea had become an accepted part of the working man's leisure. Blackpool began to welcome the industrial north. And for those who could afford to put money by, the delights of continental travel became a possibility. There was a spirit of restlessness, of adventure in the air, sitting uneasily alongside the remains of romantic melancholia. For some it was Kipling who expressed the new feeling when he 'invited them to jump from Streatham to east of Suez, and roam with him the Seven Seas – in imagination'.[2] But for others it was the music hall, always first to catch the faintest whiff of anything topical:

A cycling club outing at the turn of
the century

Bathing strengthens the interlect, braces the body, clears the system, puts new life in the blood, old heads on to young shoulders, fills the pocket, drives away care, cures, corns, warts, bunions, Pilgrims' progresses, water on the brain, *new*-ralgia, *old*-ralgia, velocipedes, bicycles, telephones, tellacrams, and all the Primrose 'Ills as flesh is heir to . . .[3]

Blackpool beach, the Tower and the funfair – the playground of the industrial north – in about 1896, and the environment in which the music hall flourished

Other shores beckoned too, not only in imagination. With the growing industrial might of Germany and the United States hovering above the horizon, a new interest in the British Empire quickened into life and prompted hordes of eager settlers to chance their luck in places undreamt of before. A cheap and efficient postal service carried home so many vivid descriptions of an exotic way of life that many members of the government knew less of what was happening in the world at large than did thousands of lower-middle-class families.

The theatre was not left out of the rush. *The Era*, the theatrical trade journal of the time, is full of items telling the adventures of troupes playing in South Africa or Australia or India. The voyage from Liverpool to New York had been clipped to seven days as early as 1885, and this was partly responsible for the large numbers of British

Albert Chevalier and Florence Turner in *My Old Dutch* in 1915. The film was based on his famous song of the same name. Many music-hall artistes and their routines were featured in films around this time

artistes either appearing in straight theatre or playing vaudeville in the United States. Names like Albert Chevalier, Gus Elen and Dan Leno were common currency among a large section of the American public, and *The Era* was diligent in recording how high was the esteem in which they were held. 'Chevalier anecdotes and the Chevalier physiognomy have occupied a considerable portion of space in the New York newspapers ever since it was announced that Koster and Bial had finally secured this wonderful artist, and that he had sailed for these shores.'[4]

Unfortunately there was an ugly side to all this ebullience. Imperialism could not but drag to the surface its vicious twin, militant nationalism, and popular stages throughout the country from 1895 onwards exhibited leading entertainers strutting to choruses of songs like 'Soldiers of the Queen'. This was a far cry from the days when working or lower-middle-class families had looked upon one of their members becoming a professional soldier with a sense of shame, or even of disgrace. The music hall had never been naïve, especially about the glories of war, and a healthy strain of scepticism had always run through its attitude towards politics and politicians. When the famous 'By Jingo' song of 1878 swept the country and was honoured by being quoted in Parliament and enshrined in a *Times* leader, there were at

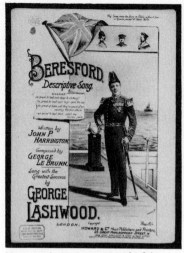

Two patriotic songs typical of the
kind popular in music-hall
programmes

least two debunking parodies running at the same time. The original
words, which went like this:

> We don't want to fight, but by Jingo if we do,
> We've got the ships, we've got the men,
> And got the money too.
> We've fought the bear before, and while we're Britons true,
> The Russians shall not have Constantinople;

were changed to:

> I don't want to fight, I'll be slaughtered if I do;
>> I'll change my togs, I'll sell my kit,
>> And pop my rifle too;
>> I don't like the war, I ain't a Briton true;
>> And I'll let the Russians have Constantinople;

or

>> Newspapers talk of Russian hate,
>> Of its ambition tell,
>> Of course they want a war because
>> It makes the papers sell.
>> Let all the politicians
>> Who desire to help the Turk
>> Put on the uniform themselves
>> And go and do the work.

But when in 1895 Dr Jameson and 600 troopers marched on Johannesburg to protect 'the women and children' and ignominiously surrendered to the Boers almost at once, patriotism went mad, and sketches, songs and recitations drenched the music-hall bills. At the Tivoli, for example, where one member of the audience had brought along his own Union Jack and waved it throughout a performance of a song dedicated to Dr Jameson, pandemonium broke loose.

> At the concluding verse the national flag was lowered from the flies; and when the singer retired there was a scene of wild enthusiasm. The Union Jack wielder's example, as it were, set the heart of the audience aflame. Hats were waved, handkerchiefs fluttered from the boxes, and above the deafening cheering could be heard the magic words 'Rule Britannia'. Taking its cue from the audience, the orchestra began to play, the audience stood and sang, the chorus was repeated again and again until, too exhausted to go on, everyone trooped to the bar where, the Union Jack waver, covered in glory, received the personal congratulations of several members of the audience.[5]

It is probable that the fever might have abated much earlier had not the Kaiser sent a telegram of congratulation to the leader of the Boers. When England heard of it, the public's temperature rose even higher and could not be finally cooled until the blunders of the South African war and the horrors of the First World War applied an effective cold compress. Inevitably the wound to Anglo-German relations went deep and the race for armaments, especially naval armaments, began in earnest. Nearly every year from 1895 to 1914 was clouded by a war or the fear of it. A frightening number of popular songs followed the trend and goaded the public into even more displays of patriotic fervour. When the *Dreadnought* was launched – thought to be the biggest battleship ever known – 'Sons of the Sea' almost accompanied it down the slipway, with its adjuration to do 'something about it' and its chorus of 'they can't build the boys of the bulldog breed' ringing out like a hymn.

Not only the popular stage shared in the general belligerence. From about 1903 the idea of a German invasion held a strange fascination for the reading public. In his novel *The Riddle of the Sands*, published in that year, Erskine Childers had first raised the spectre. 'Impregnably based on vast territorial resources which we cannot molest, the dim instincts of her people not merely directed but anticipated by the genius of her ruling houses, our great trade rival of the present, our great naval rival of the future, she grows and strengthens and waits . . .' Later, London was regaled with the sight of sandwich men dressed in the grey uniform of the Prussian soldier advertising a novel entitled *The Invasion of 1910* which put Childers's idea into much blunter language and ran as a serial in the *Daily Mail*, at that time boasting a circulation of over half a million. The fashion also invaded the theatre, and in 1909 a play by Guy Du Maurier, *An Englishman's Home*, about an invasion by 'the Emperor of the North', opened at Wyndham's and ran for eighteen months.

It was indeed a time for sensationalism, the flowering of the Yellow Press and the birth of the *Yellow Book*, the exploits of Jack the Ripper and the trial of Oscar Wilde. The 1890s produced a glut of magazines and periodicals on a scale never experienced either before or since. The two Education Acts of 1870 and 1880, in introducing a wider public to the magic of the written word, left it vulnerable to the enchantment of

> magazine supermen, drawn with varying degrees of skill, detectives and criminals, sea captains and banditti, vivified mummies and nondescript mystery men, but all alike in their strength and silence, their practical omnipotence, and omniscience in pursuit of ends often the most trivial. There was the still lower form of standardized melodrama, in which the charms of blonde and submissive virgins are perpetually the reward of blameless fools in conflict with super-subtle villainy.[6]

The Lumière Brothers' famous film of the arrival of a train at La Ciotat station in 1895 showed the potential power of the moving picture

In this atmosphere anything novel was bound to be a success, and though the exhibitions presented by two gentlemen in different London lecture halls on 20 February 1896 would hardly seem to promise enough drama for those days, consisting as they did of such items as 'The arrival of a train and debarkation of passengers at a railway station', or 'Rough sea at Dover', what they lacked in content they made up for in method of presentation. Mr Trewey at the Polytechnic and Mr R. W. Paul at the Finsbury Technical College brought before a spellbound audience the full wonders of the cinematograph, the solution to the ageless problem of capturing life in movement. No matter that what the audiences saw could be seen at first hand almost as soon as they left the hall; the fascination was in the image itself. Enthused *The Era*:

> The cinematographe is sure to be the talk of the town. Monday's audience applauded it lustily, and so enthusiastic did they become that two of the living and moving pictures were reproduced – viz. the arrival of a train and debarkation of passengers at a railway

Mr C. Goodwin Norton and his son with their hand-cranked projector. Notice the formality of dress and posture: an attempt to bring the same respectability to 'animated photographs' as he had brought to his magic-lantern entertainments

station, a wonderful illusion, and really funny, and 'The Bathers' –
a number of men luxuriating in a bath on the shores of the Mediter-
ranean ... Of course, the possibilities of such an invention as the
cinematographe are practically endless, and the British public have
now a new toy of which they are not likely soon to tire.[7]

The toy appeared under a number of guises – the Animatograph,
the Bioscope, the Matagraph, the Photo-Rotoscope, and many others.
It invaded the music halls, sometimes snatching top billing, sometimes

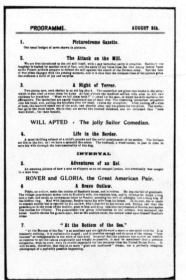

The Bioscope began its commercial
life as a 'chaser' in the music hall, but
as soon as specially built 'picture
palaces' appeared it was the music-
hall artiste who took second place.
The 1906 Palace Theatre of Varieties
programme also included Fred
Karno's *Mumming Birds*, the show in
which Chaplin was to appear three
years later as the drunken dude

being used as a 'chaser' to hurry out a sluggish audience. It began to appear at the fairground, where ornate, mechanical organs or a parade of girls and dwarfs ushered the curious into a large, draughty marquee. Scenes from the top of a tram, the front of a train, the banks of the Ganges, the Diamond Jubilee, a clog-dancing contest or life under the microscope were received with equally wild enthusiasm. When R. W. Paul filmed the Derby, which was won by the Prince of Wales's horse, Persimmon, developed it overnight and showed it the next day, the excitement was so intense that he had to run it again and again until the audience was satiated.

Newsreels, too, were met with equal fervour, the Boer War providing a ready supply of suitably patriotic images. However, indiscriminate enthusiasm walks hand-in-hand with gullibility, and the time was ripe for fraud. Few bothered to question the authenticity of films showing a squadron of Boers engaged in battle or the San Francisco earthquake at its peak, though the one was the French army on manoeuvres and the other a toy city destroyed in a corner of the studio. There was simply no time to pause and think about such things, the appetite was too enormous.

A typical 'picture palace' in 1911. Again the formality of the staff is an attempt to give the cinema the respectability of the legitimate theatre

A frame enlargement from *Tillie's Punctured Romance* (Keystone, 1914) showing the inside of an early cinema – probably a converted hall. The film is being shown with a piano accompaniment. This is the scene where Charlie and Mabel go to the cinema and see a film about a couple who have, like them, just stolen some money

Almost anything that was empty was seen as a potential cinema. Shops, barns, stables were taken over, a sheet was suspended at one end or a rough rectangle whitewashed on a wall, wooden benches or up-turned fruit boxes placed in front of it, a jangly upright piano to the side of it and a hand-cranked projector at the back of the audience. All sorts of discomforts were put up with.

In one show at Hackney the shop was so long the projector's feeble beam could not throw the whole distance, and the screen, dipped in water to make it translucent, was mid-way down the premises. The patrons who occupied seats on the same side as the projector paid a penny but those on the far side, who saw the same picture reversed, were admitted for a half-penny. As the latter could not read the subtitles [*sic*] which appeared backwards to them, they would shout to the people on the other side to read them aloud.[8]

The crowds who flocked to these 'penny gaffs', as they were called, and who wept and cheered and brawled and laughed with their screen heroes and heroines, were every bit as dedicated as those who had paid perhaps a thousand times more to hear Caruso at Covent Garden. And their demands were even more insistent. Gaumont put up studios at Loughborough where music-hall stars like Harry Lauder sang in rough synchronization to a record, and Cecil M. Hepworth converted a large house at Walton-on-Thames into a stage and labora-tory, producing films to such a high standard that he was able to export from ten to thirty copies to the United States each week. Eventually, in

1906, the Bioscope opened its doors, offering a luxury lounge and a programme of newsreels and shorts twenty minutes to half an hour long. Three years later the Provincial Cinematography Theatre Circuit flung its first loop across the country. The days of the penny gaff were numbered and the *Bioscope*, the trade magazine, wrote:

> The opening of so many theatres de luxe, with their comfortable seats, cosy appearance, and high class show of films, has sounded the death-knell of the penny picture show, which will, except in the very poorest districts, soon be as dead as a door-nail.[9]

The film had arrived as a formidable mass entertainment.

### 3. References

1. B. W. Tuchman, *The Proud Tower*, London: Hamish Hamilton, 1966.
2. David Thomson, *England in the Nineteenth Century*, London: Jonathan Cape, 1964.
3. Music-hall patter from 1942, quoted in Alan Delgado, *Victorian Entertainment*, New York: American Heritage Press, 1971.
4. *The Era*, 4 April 1896.
5. *The Era*, 18 January 1896.
6. Wingfield Stratford, *History of British Civilization*, 2 vols., London: Routledge, 1928.
7. *The Era*, 14 March 1896.
8. Leslie Wood, *The Miracle of the Movies*, London: Burke Publishing Co., 1947.
9. *The Bioscope*, quoted in John Montgomery, *Comedy Films*, London: Allen & Unwin, 1954.

# Four

'A city is, properly speaking, more poetic even than a countryside, for while nature is a chaos of unconscious forces, a city is a chaos of conscious ones. The crest of the flower or the pattern of the lichen may or may not be significant symbols. But there is no stone in the street and brick in the wall that is not actually a deliberate symbol – a message from some man, as much as if it were a telegram or a post card' – G. K. Chesterton (1901)

It was no coincidence that the rise of the cinema paralleled almost exactly the growing power of the people it entertained. The city nurtured the cinema and it was the city that fermented the industrial unrest of the last years of Victoria's reign and led to the labouring poor organizing themselves into a political force. From a countryside made almost redundant in the great drive for commercial conquest which characterized the age, many thousands of agricultural workers flocked to the city seeking secure employment and more efficient charity. As far as the speed of urban growth was concerned, Britain stood second to none, and by the time of Victoria's death in 1901 the country could classify three quarters of the population as being town-dwellers. The most powerful magnet of all Britain's cities was London. One fifth of the entire population of England and Wales lived within her boundaries in an unplanned, hopeless muddle, 'a variety of heights and eye-levels, a profusion of noises and smells, a social disorder with districts of deprivation and ostentation, and every architectural style past and present, to add to the confusion'.[1]

Largely the creation of the middle classes, London mirrored their incredible but blinkered mercantile drive, and consequently their apparent callousness, though they would have been bewildered at the charge, being nothing if not sentimental. However, the demure salon audience who could be touched by a ballad such as:

> Underneath the gaslight's glitter,
> Stands a little fragile girl,
> Heedless of the night winds bitter,
> As they round about her whirl;[2]

could also tolerate the slums in which that girl tried to survive. And not only tolerate them, but positively defend them as a necessary foundation for Britain's prosperity. Better homes for workers, ran the argument, implied higher salaries in order to pay the rent, which could only lead to a rise in the price of exports and a resultant loss of precious foreign markets. No one chose to remind the advocates of the theory that Britain's foreign markets had remained unchallenged for years. So the slums were allowed to proliferate, swollen with the destitute thousands fleeing the countryside, until living in London became uncomfortable, not to say hazardous, for the middle-class families living within a stone's-throw of them. One could never tell when one was going to be physically assaulted by a drunkard or morally affronted by 'the squalid throng of homeless, wretched outcasts, sleeping on benches', which Arthur Ponsonby, son of a noble family, could see every night as he walked from Westminster to Waterloo Bridge.

He became a Socialist, but for others the step was not so drastic. They solved the slum problem by fleeing from it and creating those enclaves of respectability in the outer suburbs which were so marked a feature of Victorian London. The houses they abandoned, substantial and three or four-tiered, were ideal bait for the property agent. He wasted no time in snapping them up and renting them to the people in most need of accommodation, the homeless poor. Warren after warren came into being in this way, let and sub-let in bewildering permutations. In the 1890s, for example, half of London's dock labourers existed in homes like this, sharing one room or a part of one room. The houses crawled with vermin, running water became polluted and bred cholera, sanitation was non-existent – a piece of paper in a corner of a room serving as a lavatory – and damp and decay and filth harboured lice, the carriers of typhus, the 'poor man's disease'. Infant mortality was high throughout most of the century, but greatest among the poor and the workers where mothers had to work to live. Infants could not be fed properly, and to keep a starving child pacified there arose the pernicious practice of dosing him with opium mixtures. Some of the most moving documents of the time were written by medical officers of health fighting against heart-breaking odds and brought to the brink of despair. It was not enough to provide only drainage and pure water, they argued, the real evil was overcrowding, that 'jarring discord in the civilization we boast – a worse than pagan savageness in the Christianity we profess'. Once overcrowding was solved, the rest of society's evils would be cured.

So long as twenty, thirty, or even forty individuals are permitted – it might almost be said compelled – to reside in houses originally built for the accommodation of a single family or at most two families, so long will the evils pointed out in respect of health, of ignorance, of indecency, immorality, intemperence, prostitution, and crime continue to exist almost unchecked.[3]

'Warren after warren came into being in this way, let and sub-let in bewildering permutations.' This photograph comes from a series of lantern slides published by the League for the Prohibition of the Sale of Intoxicating Liquor to Children in Liverpool

The problem of the slums was partially solved in two ways, both of which were to make the middle-class dream of the idyllic suburb short-lived. The men who built the railways, docks, factories and new, wide streets that cut great swathes out of the city, unerringly picked on those areas which, as well as demanding the least compensation for being flattened, were also the most populous – the slums. But where were the homeless to go? Some went into municipal dwellings, but most went outwards, along the same routes as their middle-class betters, as far as their government cheap fares would allow and wherever a home could be put up for them. This was the first threat to the suburb. The second came from a much more obvious quarter, though probably an unexpected one – the middle classes themselves. They found it impossible to live in splendid isolation; they needed their attendants, their hewers of wood and drawers of water, or service industries, as they are now called, within easy calling distance. Thus during the last quarter of the century we see the spectacle of a new type of slum, the mile upon mile of workers' cottages and red-brick 'villas' hugging every railway line out of London. In time the city began to resemble an 'elephant sucking into its gorged system half the life and blood and the bone of the rural districts', as Lord Rosebery remarked.

One step up on the social ladder, and
the milieu with which Chaplin is
likely to have identified

The cost to the human spirit was high. Among the hard, ugly streets which forced their mould on everyone who lived in them there was no place for the individual. A man had to hide and protect his

'Cocking a snook': Chaplin in *Between Showers* (Keystone, 1914), and, dressed as a woman, in *The Masquerader* (Keystone, 1914). This gesture was probably learnt in the streets of Victorian London

inner life for fear of being labelled an outsider and risking social ostracism. Even the sharp wits, the humour, the perkiness which the streets could breed, could turn suddenly vicious towards anything strange or unfamiliar. Social and economic pressures tended towards standardization, in education, in building, in mass literature, in clothes. The great pride of the late Victorians was the way they measured everything: statistics became a ruling passion, and statistics implied an interest in numbers, norms, averages. Social historians and politicians began to talk about 'the masses' and leading psychologists directed their attention towards 'the herd instinct'. The more personal, intimate contacts of rural life disappeared and 'whole areas lost ordinary contact with their neighbours, and London became, in the most indulgent terms, an island of villages; in the most heartless, a geographical expression of increasing vagueness'.[4]

Humour based on personal discomfort was already the staple fare of lower-class Victorian entertainment. Chaplin continued the tradition in his films. The illustrations show a hand-painted animated lantern slide from about 1865, and a frame enlargement from *The Cure* (Mutual, 1917), with Chaplin trapping Eric Campbell's bandaged foot in a revolving door

City and countryside seemed like two different continents, and a city boy could look with amazement at the habits and standards of his country relatives as if he had strayed into a quaint museum. 'Read to them out of a newspaper and you know they'd sit there going "Ah, ah". Well they don't know anything much ... some of 'em hadn't heard of the Crimea war you know – and of course they'd all be people who was alive then.'[5]

The countryside had always figured prominently in the Victorian dream. It was natural life as opposed to the artificiality of the city. As the gulf between the two grew wider, the more fanciful grew the ideas of the joys to be found in the country. It developed into a land of innocence, of childhood, of untramelled growth, and nostalgia for its passing pervaded a great deal of Victorian thought and culture. Agricultural communities based on cooperation and 'primary emotions' started in high hopes and disintegrated in petty jealousies; some even went to the plains of America to breed the perfect rural citizen. 'The country is the symbol of God's love and care for man. All that we are and all that we have comes from it,' declaimed Ebenezer Howard in 1898, and his idea of marrying town and country inspired much lower-middle-class youth well into the twentieth century, and did at least achieve practical results in the garden cities of Welwyn and Letchworth. But for the millions of town dwellers who were not likely to see an open field more than once a year, the romantic yearnings for a mythical Arcadia lingered on in window boxes and the brave, little public parks that London is so rich in.

Most of London's other amenities were not as plentiful nor as popular. Apart from the problems of health and housing, the difficulties encountered in implementing the new Education Acts were daunting enough. Many illiterate parents resented the spread of education and banned homework, newspapers and magazines from the home in an effort to preserve their authority. They encouraged truancy. A child showing an interest in books or learning was considered 'stuck-up' and mocked by his companions. The atmosphere and standard of a school depended on the district it served. The council ones were full of stunted, pale-faced children shuffling late into assembly, or sitting listlessly at their desks, often in classes of sixty. 'He was up at five o'clock this morning, and out with the milkman on his round,' a headmaster tartly retorted, when a school visitor pointed out a particularly sleepy pupil. 'This evening he will be out selling papers. You know, these poor children are not put to bed as early as yours.'[6] If the streets were violent, the school gave formal expressions to it in savage beatings accompanied by an extraordinary amount of ritual. And the ritual was needed, for in a way not known today it played a major role in the life of the Victorian family.

It affected both high and low. The ritual of the desolate, religious Sunday, the clothes that emphasized status, the elaborate children's games, the handing out of soup to the poor, the visit of the music teacher and the dressmaker, the collecting of scraps from the butcher or fishmonger, the polite table manners – subtle checks and balances, maintaining class and keeping it distinct. But they could also bring a sense of isolation, perhaps no more so than in the notion of respect-ability, the dividing of people into the 'nice' and the 'not nice'. Every level of society except the criminal was infected with this disease, though its variants seemed endless. For example, in the family of a London navvy who was out of work for most of the year it took this form.

The children were brought up to 'raise the hat to ladies'. They were dressed in new clothes. Bedtime was strictly imposed. Grace was said at meals 'and we weren't allowed to talk over the table . . . You had to sit right and you had to hold your knife and fork right.' Cards were not allowed in the house, and although Sidney had to fetch drinks for his parents from the pub, his father 'would never take us in the public house . . . he always used to say "Nobody'll ever say I learned my children to drink".'[7]

In fact, drink and the suffering caused by it was one problem shared by all. The average life expectancy of a male was forty-four, and alcohol had a lot to do with it. The rich could drink themselves to death discreetly in the seclusion of their home, but the working man did it in the pub, and in London there were many to choose from. 'In the one mile of Whitechapel Road, from Commercial Street to Stepney Green, there were in 1899 no less than forty-eight drinking places; in the three-quarter mile stretch of the Strand from Trafalgar Square to St Clement's there were forty-six.'[8] In other words, if they had all been one side of the street, there would have been a pub every thirty-seven yards.

The pub was an essential part of the community life of the poor. As a cheaply hired meeting-place it had welcomed friendly societies, Sunday schools, burial clubs and trade unions. It always occupied a strategic position, such as a street corner or a point close by a railway station. Workmen could breakfast in it first thing in the morning and call in again on their way home at night. It was deliberately tricked out to seduce the passer-by. It boasted colourful signboards, elegant frosted glass, brilliant lamps and prettily arranged tables on the pavement outside, which in those days was alive with pedestrians. Even the

Exterior of a working-class pub in Liverpool in about 1889 from a series of photographs taken by the Liverpool photographer, F. R. Inston. The pub was usually the most inviting building in the street and attracted both the working man and his children

stiff-backed Victorians could appreciate that, in a society starved of recreation, the pub was one of the few routes open to the working man by which he could escape the unredeemed squalor of his life. Its attraction was irresistible. 'The wretched state of his home is one of the most powerful causes which induce a man to spend his money on strictly selfish gratifications: he comes home tired and exhausted; he wants quiet; he needs refreshment; filth, squalor, discomfort in every shape are around him; he naturally gets away from it if he can.'[9]

Families were broken through drink, wives left penniless, their children crazed with hunger. With the rise in wages, more was spent on it; with increasing mechanization, more could be produced and bottled; with the growing demand, more pubs could be built. 'I can get my husband, sir, past two public houses,' declared a working man's wife, 'but I cannot get him past twenty.'

Pubs became associated with crime, with the raffish sporting crowd, with prostitution. Many working men's clubs, which had begun with the avowed aim of improving their members by weaning them away from the bottle, degenerated into noisy, violent drinking-clubs which could spill their drunken revellers on to the streets as late as two o'clock in the morning. But it would be wrong to suppose that all pubs were of the same ilk. Certain of them from mid-Victorian days onwards became associated with different types of patron – medical students, officers, actors, foreigners and lawyers. Equally wrong would be the conviction that all working men drank themselves into a stupor. Among the 'respectable artisans' were many who fiercely attacked drink and swore never to touch it. Their example could influence a lower-paid worker. He needed courage, however, for the working-class attitude towards drink was laced with fears about virility or notions about generosity and good-fellowship. Anyone wishing to give it up ran the risk of ridicule and contempt.

To bolster his resolve, he could join one of the temperance societies, a misnomer if ever there was one, for in their own way they were as intemperate as the people they chose to save. They rallied support from the middle class and from the comfortable working class, from those sections of society known for their noncomformity in religion and their incapacity for pleasure. They numbered many thousands, recruited in street meetings, theatres, public halls and churches, all sworn to 'the pledge', which demanded nothing less than total abstinence. Their main targets were women and children. Posters, pamphlets, poems and songs featuring a deserted wife or an angelic child pleading with its dissipated father, plumbed some of the lowest depths of Victorian sentimentality. Capable of intense political agitation, the societies pressed local councils to ban pubs, persuaded powerful landlords to reduce the number of pubs on their estates – the Duke of Bedford's Bloomsbury estate in 1887 contained far fewer pubs than its neighbours – and played on the grievances of the working class by representing drink as the weapon of the aristocracy to keep the underprivileged dull and supine. Though their influence crept into the popular literature of the day, they never really gained the support of those they most wished to influence, mainly because they overstated their case and possibly because they could never quite make up their minds about cause and effect. Were the poor wretched because they drank or did they drink because they were wretched?

It was left for others to carry the theme more persuasively into popular literature. George R. Sims, who wrote *How the Poor Live* in 1883, had two years earlier brought out a collection of verses called the *Dagonet Ballads*, in which the horrors of drink were set against a more realistic background.

Victorian puritanism abhorred drunkenness, but gave no consideration to the conditions which caused it. This illustration comes from a lantern slide issued by the Church Army

George R. Sims's popular ballads, like 'In the Workhouse, Christmas Day', recorded the evils of Victorian life in a palatable form

Jack was a Sunday scholar, so I gathered from what he said,
But he sang in the road for a living – his father and mother were dead
And he had a drunken granny, who turned him into the street –
She drank what he earned, and often he hadn't a crust to eat.[10]

Ballads of this type were translated into song and performed to enraptured audiences on the stage of the music hall, a strange irony in as much as some of the most virulent attacks on the music hall harped on its alleged encouragement of drunkness. For most of its existence, it aimed exclusively at the working class for whom the temptations of drink were part and parcel of a hard and bitter process of growing up. Any working man, therefore, who could succumb to drink did not need the music hall to help him on his way. He would have had more than enough opportunities elsewhere. But prejudices die hard and the origins of the music hall in the free-and-easies, concerts and variety programmes organized by taverns in the early part of the nineteenth century could never be completely forgiven until the days of the respectable Palace of Varieties. In fact, once its licence to sell drink in the auditorium was removed in 1870, the music hall tended to shift the bar further and further away from the audience, so that by 1892 a Parliamentary Report could describe music halls as 'temperance halls at all times'.

Drink was merely a handy weapon. The real reason for all the criticism went much deeper and included everyone who frequented the music hall whether they drank or not. It was the atmosphere of the place that alarmed the critics. The entertainment they saw was vulgar, violent, raw and anarchic, and resurrected in a middle-class mind all its dormant fears of the mob. Nowhere else would anyone have met a more vivid and potent expression of working-class culture. In an age when the labourer was finding his political voice and discovering strength in numbers, it is not surprising to find that the music hall could be seen as a very ominous portent indeed.

By 1908 there were fifty-seven in London alone, and many more in the Northern circuits. Some of them were the resplendent, baroque creations of the West End in which the working class grew gradually more scarce as the management grew more particular; places where 'the most prominent and distinguished representatives of art, literature and the law mingled nightly with city financiers, lights of the sporting and dramatic world, and a very liberal sprinkling of the "uppercrust" as represented by the golden youth of the period'.[11] But most of them were still lowly theatres like the Bedford, where Sickert sat and peered through a fog of cheap tobacco smoke at a perspiring singer bawling out his songs 'with the glare of footlights cast up on his

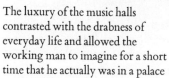

The luxury of the music halls contrasted with the drabness of everyday life and allowed the working man to imagine for a short time that he actually was in a palace

crumpled shirt front and making a dark cavern of his mouth'.[12]

While the 'legitimate' theatre, worlds away, was full of excitement about a new realism which consisted of elaborate sets peppered with genuine door handles and window frames, the music hall, in contrast, offered little in the way of scenery, but much in the way of reality. Here the working man could see his own world as he knew it, with the obdurate, harsh facts of his own street or backyard made more bearable by humour or compassion. Even when his heroes were as elegant and fastidious as the Lions Comiques, they were still of his own class and remained steadfastly loyal to it throughout their careers. Though his heroines could marry into fashion, they always understood his needs and sang about them without shame. On a Sunday morning, at a pub called the White Horse in Brixton, it was possible for a complete

Stage designers produced more and more elaborate sets in a desperate attempt to satisfy their audiences and compete with historical drama on the screen. This illustration shows Constance Collier and Beerbohm Tree in *Antony and Cleopatra* at His Majesty's Theatre, London

stranger to go up to any one of a galaxy of stars and within a few minutes be immersed in a conversation about landladies, lodgings, unemployment, cheap seaside holidays, pawnshops and the like, knowing full well that though his sympathetic listener had left behind those problems years ago, he never scorned to talk about them.

Not surprisingly, the material the performers worked with was nearly always gross, sometimes disconcerting and very often disgusting. But it was never salacious. Sly innuendo belonged to the French music hall, which had a form of censorship not known in this country that encouraged a sleight-of-hand suggestiveness which an English audience would have found offensive. By sheer breadth of personality, stars like Marie Lloyd or Dan Leno succeeded in transmuting the petty, squalid, day-to-day minutiae of the poor into a robust affirmation of living:

> They could sing a song about being found in bed with the landlady, and make it sound like the benediction at the end of a service. They could make the strait-laced feel that marital infidelity was the true faith. They could smile at you, and make you feel that there was no trouble you could not bear. They could do this because they were so wholesome . . .[13]

G. H. Chirgwin, 'the White-Eyed Kaffir', was one of Chaplin's heroes. He was well known for his risqué jokes, broad even by music-hall standards

They also worked hard for their money. It was nothing for G. H. Chirgwin, 'The White-Eyed Kaffir', to work six halls in one evening. Lottie Collins, who made 'Ta-ra-ra-boom-de-ay' so famous, flung herself into it with such abandon that at the Grand Theatre, Islington, she fell fainting in the wings. They were by no means exceptional. *The Era* recorded that one Tuesday evening a Miss Nelly Laybourn 'did two turns in London, caught the 11.50 train at Euston, and appeared in Glasgow on Wednesday, sang fourteen songs and was back in town as fresh as paint on Thursday, and worked two turns'.

In London the salaries for top performers were high. As early as 1862 Blondin was paid £100 a night for appearing at the Crystal Palace, and in the same period Leotard, 'The Man on the Flying Trapeze', was offered a halfpenny for each person attending his performance at Highbury Barn. He earned more than £100 a week playing to audiences of over 48,000. By the 1900s Dr Walford Bodie, the most colourful miracle-worker and hypnotist to appear in the halls, could demand £400 a week, and Harry Lauder £700. But the incessant travelling and snatched meals, the demanding schedules and exhausting performances, took their toll in the end, especially as most of the artistes were reared in an environment hardly celebrated for providing a comfortable and healthy childhood. Dan Leno died at forty-four, Marie Lloyd at fifty-two, Jenny Hill, 'The Vital Spark', at forty-six,

Gus Elen, the coster comedian, made famous the song 'Jack Jones' which Chaplin allegedly sung when he made his stage première at the tender age of five

'The Great Vance' at forty and George Leybourne, better known as 'Champagne Charlie', at forty-two. Perhaps the possibility of an early death haunted many top performers and was the main cause for an extravagant and febrile way of life. But it cannot totally explain their intense and sharpened awareness, for they shared this in common with all their peers.

It can be found in songs and characterizations based on meticulous and sympathetic observation. Gus Elen, a great coster singer, drew his character for a song called 'E dunno where 'E are' from a man he had seen in Covent Garden. 'My make-up for this song, I may mention, is an exact reproduction of the attire of an old chap who may be seen any day in the region of Covent Garden market. In fact I invariably model myself in this manner upon some striking type of the class I intend to portray.'[14] Studying a new song or character could be a painstaking and exhaustive business needing weeks of perfecting, and this gradually led to a sharper and more concentrated technique aimed at presenting a simplified type. What this lacked in variety it made up for in depth, and since part of the success of the music hall depended on familiar jokes or routines – what some chose to call its monotony – a comedian or singer could play one character throughout his career without any risk of becoming tiresome.

Many of the performers were trained actors who, aside from their usual routine, were capable of giving fiery recitations of Dickens or of writing their own melodramas. Some composed their own tunes and lyrics or could burlesque classical plays like *Macbeth*, indicating a surprising knowledge of the original on the part of the audience. Unaccompanied dialogue was forbidden in the music hall right up to the early years of this century (though the rule was often slackly enforced), so dumbshow and mime became an accepted part of the programme. But eventually playlets limited to a statutory half-hour were extracted from melodramas, and snippets of Shakespeare accompanied many variety bills.

In fact from its earliest days music hall purveyed a kind of twilight culture, investing in picture galleries, waxworks, museums and nude statuary – a rough compromise, perhaps, between the rowdyism of the gallery and the pretensions of the stalls. Charles Morton, 'The Father of the Halls', staged a condensed version of *The Tempest* at the Canterbury Music Hall in Westminster Bridge Road, put on opera and ballet, and was credited with introducing to London the music for Gounod's *Faust*. Comic songs, employing skilful rhymes and rhythms, must have stimulated a more imaginative use of language. Gus Elen sang one of the most famous of them:

Away went Polly
With a step so jolly
That I knew she'd win.
Down the road
The pace was killing,
But the mare was willing
For a lightning spin;
All the rest were licked
And might as well have
ne'er been born.
Woa, mare! Woa, mare!
You've earned your
little bit of corn!

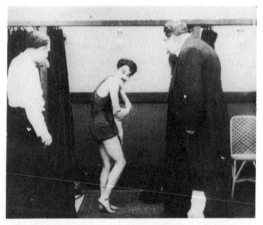

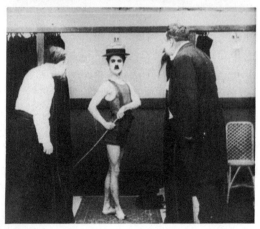

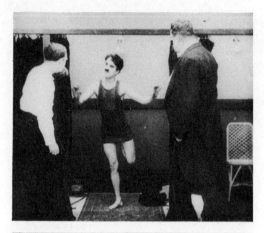

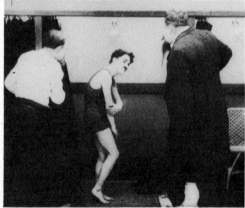

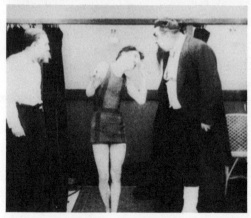

In *The Cure* (Mutual, 1917), Chaplin burlesques the 'Tableaux Vivants', a popular feature of many music-hall programmes

Not a few critics, however, looked askance at the wit, polish and 'tone' which began to infiltrate the music hall in even more strength as the nineteenth century came to an end. They bemoaned the passing of vulgarity, with its power to knock away the props supporting sentimentality or hypocrisy, they mourned the days of the intimate hall where performers and audience were almost equal contributors to the same event. When Marie Lloyd was left out of the first Variety Command Performance in 1912 because she had never sterilized her act, many thought that the golden years of the music hall were over. But the process had started earlier. People who had moved out to the suburbs lost contact with theatres they had patronized for years, and halls which stood on commanding sites had been pulled down to make way for offices.

That was by no means the whole story, however. By virtue of making the working man's life more bearable, the music hall acted as a very efficient safety valve, helping to regulate a pressure which might otherwise have erupted into violence. The critics of the music hall were right in so far as they feared the potential power of its audience; where they were wrong was to imagine that it bred revolt. The reverse was true. From the beginning of an organized trade union movement and the formation of the Independent Labour Party in 1893, the music-hall audience began slowly to change its character. The biggest demonstration of labour power, the transport strike of 1911, took place only one year before Royalty's agreement to attend a Command Performance stifled music hall with the dead hand of respectability. In other words, the more the working classes could express their grievances in action, the less they needed music hall as a release.

As the First World War drew nearer, the industrial unrest grew fiercer and seemed to infect every level of society. The Suffragettes, the Irish Question, the battles to emasculate the House of Lords, the Aliens Act to restrict immigration of foreign workers – all were symptons of a growing and bitter disillusionment with an age that seemed incapable of ordering its own affairs. One can sense a 'universal note of desperation, of hysteria, of pent-up passion',[15] as men and women tried to grapple with an apparently indifferent and remorseless fate. Science had toppled traditional beliefs and nothing seemed as cut and dried as it once had been. 'There was much that was gross and vicious in the old days, but it was not daintily arrayed,' wrote George R. Sims.[16] 'Virtue went smiling in the sunshine and vice flaunted in the gas-light, and they did not dress so much alike that it was with difficulty you could tell one from the other.'[17]

Increasingly London became the symbol of the general malaise. Since the days of Carlyle and Ruskin it had figured in writers' imaginations alongside the machines as the perfect example of the Devil's own work, but a gradual shift of emphasis took place from the 1890s onwards. Novelists began to picture it as a labyrinth in which characters engaged in a protracted search for their identity, or they invested it with a quasi-tragic poetry, a mysteriousness which Balzac and Verlaine had already explored. Both attitudes betrayed an equally strong fascination for the city which even its ugliness could not weaken. 'A plain woman is usually much more fascinating than a beautiful woman,' averred Thomas Burke, 'and London, in its sprawled and jutting formlessness, is an expression of life more moving than any planned city that obeys the bygone laws of harmony and proportion.'[18]

This attitude, however, is as suspect in its way as that of Ruskin. There is no easier way of trying to dispose of emotions that one finds difficult to assimilate than by giving them concrete form. Thus, the mournfulness, despair, confusion and deep insecurity that filled many people at the turn of the century led them to transform London into an image of themselves. But this was only one effect of the general malaise. Not only did Balfour hold it responsible for the humiliating Tory defeat of 1906, but he was also forced to conclude that it lay behind 'the same movement which has produced massacres in St Petersburg, riots in Vienna and Socialist processions in Berlin'.

Later, historians were to label it as the beginning of the age of 'the common man', a phenomenon whose ambitions, anger, hopes and defeats were crystallized for millions in the figure of the 'Little Fellow'.

## 4. References

1. Asa Briggs, *Victorian Cities*, London: Odhams Press, 1963.
2. 'Won't You Buy My Pretty Flowers?', words by A. W. French, music by G. W. Persley.
3. Second Annual Report of the Medical Officer to the Strand (1858).
4. H. J. Dyos and D. A. Reeder, 'Slums and Suburbs', in H. J. Dyos and M. Wolff (eds.), *The Victorian City. Images and Realities*, 2 vols., London: Routledge & Kegan Paul, 1973.
5. Paul Thompson, 'Voices from Within', in ibid.
6. George R. Sims (ed.), *London Life*, London: Cassell, n.d.
7. Thompson, 'Voices from Within', loc. cit.
8. B. Harrison, 'Pubs', in Dyos and Wolff (eds.), *The Victorian City*, op. cit.
9. Southwood Smith, quoted in W. J. Reader, *Victorian England*, London: Batsford, 1964.
10. George R. Sims, 'The Road to Heaven', *The Lifeboat and Other Poems*, London: J. P. Fuller, 1883.
11. C. D. Stuart and A. J. Park, *The Variety Stage: a History of Music Halls*, London: T. Fisher Unwin, 1895.
12. Max Beerbohm, 'The Blight on Music Halls', in *More*, London: Heinemann, 1922.
13. Thomas Burke, *City of Encounters*, London: Constable, 1932.
14. Gus Elen, quoted in Samuel McKechnie, *Popular Entertainment Through the Ages*, London: Sampson Low (Marston), n.d.
15. David Thomson, *England in the Nineteenth Century*, London: Jonathan Cape, 1964.
16. George R. Sims, quoted in 'Lord' George Sanger, *Seventy Years a Showman*, London: Dent, 1926.
17. Charles Chaplin, *Charlie Chaplin's Own Story*, Indianapolis: Bobbs-Merrill, 1916.
18. Burke, *City of Encounters*, op. cit.

# Five

'The saddest thing I can imagine is to get used to luxury' – Charles
Chaplin, *My Autobiography* (1964)

Modesty is not a quality ascribed to Chaplin by any of his biographers.
Instead they paint a portrait of a man wholly driven by a consuming
and insatiable ego; his son, Charles junior, calls it 'colossal'. It springs
up from the pages of Chaplin's autobiography, unadorned and un-
ashamed, and on that count, at least, the record can be said to be
accurate. There are grave doubts about the rest. In 1916 a book was
written in America entitled *Charlie Chaplin's Own Story*, which after
a brief run was withdrawn from the market. To his deep confusion
Chaplin had discovered that facts could be checked and that critics
could be as scrupulous about them as he was cavalier. Since that time
the world has learned to be very wary of what he has to say about
himself, and one might have imagined that having realized this he
would have mended his ways. But, alas, when his autobiography
appeared in 1964,[1] it merely confirmed the suspicion that he had not
changed.

   This is especially true of the section devoted to his early life. Many
vital questions are raised only to be tossed aside. Facts are surrounded
with a thick fog of sentiment. Dates are scarce. To try to keep a running
time-scale while reading *My Autobiography* is rather like having to
navigate by the stars on an overcast night. By the time one reaches the
next break in the clouds the boat may be miles off course. Certain
enigmas are not even hinted at. For example, there is still no explanation as to why his birth is not recorded in Somerset House. It may well
be that it is there under a different name, but not a hint of this appears
in his tale. Much more serious, however, is his habit of embellishment –
to use the politest term. About his father's death in St Thomas's Hospital,
he has this to say:

> The hospital wanted to know who would bury him. Mother, not
> having a penny, suggested the Variety Artists' Benevolent Fund, a
> theatrical charity organization. This caused an uproar with the

Chaplin side of the family – the humiliation of being buried by charity was repugnant to them. An Uncle Albert from Africa, my father's youngest brother, was in London at the time and said he would pay for the burial.[2]

He then goes into the description of a funeral held on a mournful, drizzling day, complete with all the necessary middle-class trappings of grief.

As a matter of fact, Charles Chaplin senior was buried on 13 May 1901 in grave No. 577 B3 com., a common or pauper's grave, in Lambeth cemetery. It would seem that Uncle Albert did not pay for his brother's funeral after all, and that the horse-drawn carriages, the flowers on the coffin, the satin round the corpse, the wreaths thrown into the grave and the black-bordered handkerchief that followed them – in fact the whole scene from beginning to end – are pieces of straight fiction. The natural reaction is to ask why. What made Chaplin go to such lengths to avoid the reality? It could have been his need to dramatize, but then it might be argued that a pauper's funeral gives more scope for the tragic muse than a standard burial. Might it be that he was never there, that he had not the slightest interest in seeing his father interred? Perhaps Mr Chaplin had been completely disowned by everyone and his son was ashamed to admit it years later. Perhaps he wasn't his father after all ... and so on. The alternatives appear numberless.

Charles Chaplin Snr died on 10 May 1901 at the age of thirty-seven. The cause of death was cirrhosis of the liver, a disease usually associated with alcoholism. His wife's address, 16 Golden Place, Chester Street, Lambeth, is interesting. Even in those days it was quite a good street in which to live

The shadow this kind of flaw casts over the rest of the book cannot be ignored. Short of having to answer the classic conundrum 'A Cretan once said that all Cretans are liars. Can we believe him?' it places the reader in the position of having to verify every single event at its source – a patently impossible task, in as much as most of the people involved are dead. Certain facts, obviously, are indisputable and common knowledge, but more interesting than the facts themselves is the way Chaplin deals with them. They are incorporated in a narrative which, for a man who has always made a great point of his powers of observation, is singularly lacking in intimate, personal detail. Reading it is like trying to recall a forgotten name which is on the tip of one's tongue, or like looking through an unfocused lens at images whose outlines blur and swim in front of the eyes and yet whose shapes are mysteriously familiar. Isn't there a scene like this somewhere in Dickens; doesn't that phrase recall a famous saying; isn't this an episode out of a silent film? It is altogether too diffuse, too typical of what one would expect of someone who had read about the late Victorian era rather than lived it. To put it shortly, the core is missing.

Perhaps his early life was more conventional and dull than he cares to reveal. Until he was five he lived in comfort. Poverty, when it

Really poor children at the time of
Chaplin's youth would have been
dressed like this

Chaplin, aged seven, in a photograph taken at the Hanwell Schools for Orphans and Destitute Children (Cuckoo Schools) where he resided for eighteen months. Even in the poorhouse he seemed better off than the children in the previous illustration

came, only lasted three or four years, after which he was in almost continuous work. Even the workhouse and orphanage he was sent to would have been nothing like as terrifying as at the beginning of Victoria's reign. They supplied meat and fresh milk every day and provided a balanced diet many poor people nowadays would be grateful to receive. Of course, there must have been periods of near-starvation when his mother was in the asylum and his brother at sea; moments of despair, of loneliness, hopelessness, of biting shame, but they did not last for ever. Yet Chaplin never brings us any relief, never shows any of the jauntiness of the 'Little Fellow', nothing of his panache. And this brings us to the last and possibly most baffling aspect of the book. It contains hardly any humour. On the contrary, Chaplin seems to have gone out of his way to suppress any suggestion that in his early years he found anything to laugh about, which could not have been true. One is even more inclined to believe, therefore, that he shaped the story to be more in keeping with the role of a philospher than of a comedian.

The one light touch is given by his mother, and as she was the paramount influence in his life, any attempt to elucidate Chaplin's behaviour might well start with her. She was a music-hall artiste like

Charles Chaplin Snr was a star in his own right, and wrote several popular songs. He was better known than Chaplin's mother, a soubrette who worked the halls under the name Lily Harley

his father, gay, charming, a keen mimic, flighty and capricious. Yet though Chaplin spends a great deal of time talking about her in his autobiography, she emerges not as a person of real flesh and blood, but more like a wraith not quite making real contact with either her son or the life around her. Chaplin never calls her 'my mother', always 'Mother' – not a very positive way of expressing close and warm love. He seems to be standing aside, watching and observing her plight, more concerned with his own sadness or grief or loneliness than with the plight itself. This is not to say that he had no love for her, but it was a love that turned in upon itself, that had to generate its own heat to keep itself alive. It created images to worship and moments to mull over and dramatize. Chaplin was once quoted as saying that mother love is the only love that lasts. 'But,' says his son, Charles,

I don't think he was ever convinced that he had truly possessed that love. He frequently told the outside world that it was poverty that had caused all his childhood unhappiness, but to my maternal grandmother he admitted an even deeper source of hurt, a feeling that his mother had failed him when he had needed her most.[3]

# Chronology

It is virtually impossible to complete an accurate and comprehensive picture of Chaplin's life up till the point when he made his first film. His own biography contains few dates, and is often inaccurate in relation to events which can be checked. The following is an attempt to place in chronological order information which has been verified, and unsubstantiated evidence which does not conflict with it and which has the ring of truth.

1864　Charles Chaplin Snr born

1867　Hannah Hill born

1885　Charles Chaplin Snr's first appearance as a professional entertainer
　　　Hannah Hill goes to South Africa with a Jewish bookmaker named Hawkes
　　　A son, Sydney, is born as a result of this relationship

1886　Hannah and Sydney return from South Africa
　　　27 May: Hannah Hill (using her stage name, Lily Harley) appears at the South London Palace

1889　16 April: Charles Chaplin born

1892　Guy and Wheeler Dryden Jnr born as a result of a liaison between Hannah and Wheeler Dryden

1894　Charles Chaplin Jnr sings Jack Jones at the Canteen, Aldershot, when Lily Harley's voice fails

1896　29 May: Charles Chaplin Snr sings descriptive songs at the Paragon
　　　18 June: Charles Chaplin admitted to Cuckoo Schools, Hanwell
　　　Summer: John Willie Jackson forms the Lancashire Lads
　　　12 December: Charles Chaplin Snr sings at Oxford

1897　Fred Kitchen joins the Karno Company

1898　18 January: Charles Chaplin leaves the Cuckoo Schools, Hanwell
　　　Summer: The Lancashire Lads become the Eight Lancashire Lads
　　　12 December: Charles Chaplin appears with the Eight Lancashire Lads

1899　Charles Chaplin appears with the Eight Lancashire Lads in Sunderland

1900　1 January: Charles Chaplin appears in *Giddy Ostend* at the London Hippodrome
　　　Charles Chaplin's last appearance with the Eight Lancashire Lads at the Star Palace, Barrow
　　　Charles Chaplin plays a street waif in the tour of *From Rags to Riches*
　　　26 December: Charles Chaplin takes the part of a cat in *Cinderella* at the London Hippodrome

1901　13 April: *Cinderella* ends
　　　13 May: Charles Chaplin Snr dies
　　　Hannah Hill admitted to Cane Hill Asylum
　　　Charles Chaplin sent to Hern Boys College

1903　January: Hannah Hill leaves Cane Hill Asylum
　　　May: Charles Chaplin leaves Hern Boys College
　　　6 July: Chaplin plays Sam, the newsboy, in *Jim; A Romance of Cockayne* at the Royal Court Theatre, Kingston upon Thames

18 July: *Jim; A Romance of Cockayne* closes at the Grand Theatre, Fulham
27 July: Chaplin plays Billy in *Sherlock Holmes* for the first time
Christmas: Charles and Sydney Chaplin play in *Sherlock Holmes* at the
Theatre Royal, Dewsbury

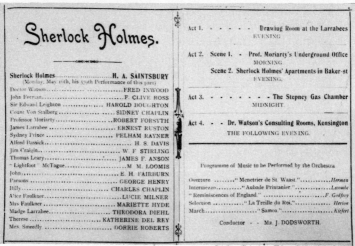

The famous actor H. A. Saintsbury gave Chaplin his first legitimate role as Sam, the newsboy, in *Jim; A Romance of Cockayne*. The play opened at Kingston upon Thames on 6 July 1903, and closed a few miles away at Fulham thirteen days later. He then cast Chaplin as Billy in *Sherlock Holmes*, a four-act drama by Arthur Conan Doyle and the American actor-writer William Gillette. It went on tour in July 1903. The above programme, dated 16 May 1904, comes from the Theatre Royal, Bradford

1904 February: Chaplin plays in *Sherlock Holmes* at the Theatre Royal, York
16 May: Chaplin plays in *Sherlock Holmes* at the Theatre Royal, Bradford
11 June: *Sherlock Holmes* tour ends at the Royal West London Theatre
27 December: Chaplin plays a wolf in *Peter Pan* at the Duke of York's Theatre, London
1905 January: New tour of *Sherlock Holmes* starts. Kenneth Rivington plays Holmes. Chaplin still plays Billy.
April: Frohman's Midland Company's tour of *Sherlock Holmes* ends at the New Theatre, Ealing
May: Third tour of *Sherlock Holmes* begins. Chaplin still plays Billy, and is the only member of the original company still in the cast
25 September: Chaplin leaves the cast of *Sherlock Holmes* at the Court Theatre, Warrington
3 October: Chaplin takes the part of Billy in *The Painful Predicament of Sherlock Holmes*, at the Duke of York's Theatre, London
14 October: *The Painful Predicament of Sherlock Holmes* closes
17 October: Chaplin plays Billy in a revival of *Sherlock Holmes* at the

Duke of York's Theatre, London. H. A. Saintsbury plays the part of Holmes

December: *Sherlock Holmes* closes at the Duke of York's Theatre, London

Chaplin was still on tour with *Sherlock Holmes* in September 1905 when he was called back to London to take the part of Billy in a ten-minute chaser written by William Gillette to accompany his play *Clarice*, which opened at the Duke of York's Theatre on 3 October 1905. However, the main play was not a success and the programme was taken off on 14 October

*Clarice* was replaced three days later on 17 October with the well-tried *Sherlock Holmes*. Once again, Chaplin played the part of Billy. After its London run, it went on tour for the second time. Chaplin left the company on 5 March 1906. He was now so well known that he received a sizeable entry in the *Green Room Book, or Who's Who on the Stage* for 1906, and even had an agent. Saintsbury's protection had served him well

1906   1 January: Chaplin, still playing Billy, starts another tour of *Sherlock Holmes* at the Grand Theatre, Doncaster

5 March: Chaplin leaves the *Sherlock Holmes* tour

14 May: Chaplin appears in *Casey's Court* at the Bradford Empire

21 May: Chaplin appears in *Casey's Circus* at Olympia, Liverpool

6 August: Chaplin appears in *The Casey Circus* at Richmond Theatre

1907   20 July: *The Casey Circus* ends its tour at Sadler's Wells

14 September: Chaplin plays a rag-and-bone man in Karno's *London Suburbia*

Although his salary remained the same, £2 10s. (£2.50) a week, Chaplin cannot have been overjoyed when he commenced his tour of *Casey's Court*, a loose story about Cockney slum children, at the Bradford Empire in the week beginning 14 May 1906. Harry Cardle, its producer, was not in the same class as Saintsbury and Gillette. He never had an entry in the *Green Room Book* again

1908   3 February: Chaplin first plays Stiffy, the Goalkeeper, in *The Football Match* at the London Coliseum

June: Chaplin appears in *Mumming Birds* at the Folies Bergères in Paris

1909   Chaplin, under contract to Karno since February 1908, plays in the Second Company versions of most of Karno's shows. These included: *The G.P.O.*, *Mumming Birds*, *The Yap-Yaps* and *Skating* (written by his brother Sydney)

1910   25 April: Chaplin plays Jimmy in *Jimmy the Fearless, or the Boy 'Ero* at the Stratford Empire

3 September: Tour of *Jimmy the Fearless* ends at the Bradford Empire.

3 October: Chaplin opens at the Colonial Theatre, New York, in *The Wow-Wows* in the part of the Hon. Archibald Binks

1911   March: Chaplin appears in *A Night in an English Music Hall* (the American title for *Mumming Birds*) at the Empress Theater, Chicago

April: Chaplin appears in the same show at the American Theater, New York

June: Chaplin appears in the same show in San Francisco

Chaplin (second from left) on board ship bound for the United States to begin a tour with the Karno second company. They opened at the Colonial Theater, New York, on 3 October 1910 in *The Wow-Wows*, a kind of variety show. The company included (extreme right) Arthur Jefferson, better known as Stan Laurel, and next to him Albert Austin, who later appeared in all Chaplin's Mutual films

Three photographs taken during the second Karno company's tour of the United States. The first, dated March 1911, shows the Empress Theater, Chicago, where the company played *A Night in an English Music Hall* (known in Britain as *Mumming Birds*). The second, taken about one month later, shows the company on the way to the West Coast. And the third, dated June 1911, finds them in San Francisco

1912 June: Chaplin returns to Britain for the summer
Summer: Chaplin tours France and the Channel Islands with a Karno company
December: Chaplin goes back to the United States

1913 September: Chaplin appears in *A Night in an English Music Hall* at the Empress Theater, Los Angeles
28 November: Chaplin gives his last performance with the Karno Company at the Empress Theater, Kansas City

Article from *Everybody's Weekly* for 7 March 1931 on the occasion of Chaplin's visit to Britain. The text is uninteresting, but the two photographs accompanying it were taken during his tour of America

This sense of betrayal seems to have influenced his dealings with all the women he became involved with. By turns jealous, selfish, ruthless and fulsomely romantic, he was always on his guard against them and they were a constant source of disquiet. Goaded by a despotic fear of rejection and betrayal, it was impossible for him to accept anything less than complete commitment, like a diver teetering on the end of the topmost board, not trusting the depth of the water. His first teenage love, Hetty, was pressed to make a declaration of her passion after only a few hours of their knowing each other. When the bewildered girl, somewhat naturally in the circumstances, replied that she could not be sure of her feelings, he immediately lapsed into a pose reminiscent of some of the more cloying moments of his screen character. 'I took her hand and patted it tenderly. "Good-bye, it's better this way. Already you have too much power over me." '4

Torn between his desperate need for love and his fear of loving in return, he wavered like a drunken man from woman to woman. Always he feared for his loss of power over them, confessing to his cameraman over many years that he was worried about his sexual potency. His ideal woman might possibly have been one who was mature and accommodating towards his moods and obsessions, a mistress and mother substitute at the same time. But maturity was not something Chaplin could readily face. It betokened control, caution, a sense of proportion and a knowledge of the rules of the game. He must have instinctively known that sooner or later he would have come off second best, completely at the mercy of emotions he could no more restrain than a child its fear of the dark. His demands would grow more insistent and importunate. The control of the relationship, so necessary for his ego, would slip out of his hands. The woman might tire of him, be bored by him, call him a child, compare him with past lovers who were more understanding. Whatever his imaginings, it is certain that mature women figured in his affairs hardly ever if at all.

His interest was invariably quickened by girls much younger than himself. It is possible that he thought of his fame and wealth as his strongest weapons, helping to awe a young girl into being sufficiently pliable. The ones he chose to play opposite him had little or no acting experience. As well as being attractive, they were also eager to learn, which made his job of moulding them to his taste that much easier. They were driven mercilessly, albeit with a great deal of charm and patience. To the outside world they were living proof that Chaplin knew all about women and how to manage them, but to the man himself they could have been the only way of turning fantasy into fact. Having dominated and manipulated a girl on a film set until she became utterly dependent on him, he could then feel safe to carry over the arrangement into real life. Unfortunately he found that the method did not always work. They were not so untutored in the ways of the world as he had imagined; careers meant more to them than domesticity and, most important, they were incapable of mothering him.

Many of Chaplin's leading ladies bore a marked similarity to his mother, and their roles often required them to perform the sort of dance routines she might have included in her act. Here we see Georgia Hale in *The Gold Rush* (Chaplin–United Artists, 1925); Myrna Kennedy in *The Circus* (Chaplin–United Artists, 1928); and Paulette Goddard in *Modern Times* (Chaplin–United Artists, 1936)

One of the least engaging things about him was the way he quite deliberately set about attracting his women. His technique was to create a kind of forlorn mood, not difficult to achieve in the period of disillusionment between the two world wars. Once accomplished, it conjured up all sorts of Byronic nuances – a man alone searching for the unattainable, a poetic soul bruised against life's rocks, beauty swamped by boorishness, innocence destroyed by cynicism. It played on past regrets, adolescent yearnings and childhood hurts, and it never failed to arouse a strong desire to protect and sympathize. 'In your dance you seem to express an exotic loneliness,' he said to a dancer in Berlin; 'to be in pursuit of some strange beauty. This quality is part of your real personality.' She couldn't fail to respond, and he continues, ' "G" took my hand. Hesitating to find words she replied, "Charlie, I love you – you're so appreciative. Although we may never meet again, I will not regret it. For we have met in our pilgrimage." '[5]

His pilgrimage was doubtless not the same as hers, for whereas she was heading towards a future, he was in flight from his past. With his growing acclaim among intellectuals, he was finding his cockney shadow an encumbrance. Yet try as he would he could never quite divest himself of it. It appeared in the midst of his riches, in public as well as in private. 'My prodigious sin was, and still is, being a non-conformist,' he avows, but having set aside a natural scepticism when confronted with such a claim, one does find on closer examination that the non-conformity is largely imaginary, falling, alas, into an all too predictable pattern. His mother must be held partly responsible, for in spite of escaping into the comparative licence of the music hall she still trailed some of the priorities of the lower middle class and handed them down to her son. Obviously sensitive to the social stigma attached to bad diction, she made determined efforts to improve her son's accent, not with unqualified success for, according to Burke,[6] whenever Chaplin was excited or agitated he lapsed into the cockney's unmistakable twang. She took pride in parading him in his Sunday best and in serving the obligatory Sunday joint. When neither ritual could survive the march of poverty, she did her best to hide the shameful fact from her neighbours. She took up religion and regaled her son with pathetic stories from the Bible or acted out scenes from the religious plays then current. Above all, with her descriptions of her music-hall successes, her tales of an idyllic life in distant South Africa, her fantasy about Sydney's alleged aristocratic father and, finally, her insistence that her sons were not 'the ordinary products of poverty, but unique and distinguished', she filled Charles with the conviction that he was meant for better things.

No wonder, then, if he constantly had to reassure himself that whatever people thought of him they must never judge him as commonplace, a word which seemed to hold untold terrors for him. The crowd, the masses, were his natural enemies, however much he liked to identify himself with the underdog. Relishing their praise, he could yet be contemptuous of it. 'When those crowds come round me like that,' he once exclaimed to Thomas Burke, 'sweet as it is to me personally – it makes me sick.'[7] The ones to whom he owed the greater part of his success were also the ones who reminded him too vividly of what he once had been. In his headlong escape from the commonplace, he charmed, entertained, shocked, ingratiated himself – anything to avoid the ignominy of leaving a blank in people's minds.

With that in view, one is inclined to believe that his espousal of liberal causes and his friendship for left-wing activists was motivated in part by his desire to stand out from the crowd. Disgust with war – something he felt deeply – was quite understandable in one who had been wearied by its excesses on the stage of the music hall. Patriotism he believed to be a luxury which only those who had had a secure childhood could afford. But when it came to a question of genuine reforming zeal, Chaplin became lukewarm. Little of his money found its way into left-wing coffers, and none of his statements went beyond a worthy belief in love for humanity and justice for all. He was once actually called 'the darling of the capitalist class'. Having preached the glories of opening a Second Front to a mass audience, he was in doubt whether he had been fired by the rightness of the cause or 'stimulated by the actor in me and the reaction of a live audience'.[8] Even he was aware of his need to impress.

Perhaps it was this obsession that saved him in the end – that and his talent. Without his crusade for a lost birthright, as it were, his environment might have swallowed him up. Surviving it, however, did not necessarily mean nullifying it. The periods of poverty, short though they may have been, left their mark. The progressively worse slums he had to live in, the abjectness of relying on parish relief, the clinging taint of the soup kitchen, the disease and malnutrition that glared out of the mutilated faces of some of the people he worked with, the torpor of unemployment – all fused into the blazing belief that poverty was the ultimate fall from grace and wealth the golden redeemer. 'I found poverty neither attractive nor edifying,' he proclaims. 'It taught me nothing but a distortion of values, an over-rating of the virtues and graces of the rich, and the so-called upper classes.'[9]

Not the automatic reaction of a non-conformist, one might conclude, even with its implication that he has seen the error of his ways. Rather more is it typical of the pervasive materialism of late Victorian London and the aspirations of its lower middle class. As soon as he could afford to, he indulged those aspirations to the full. He took a flat and furnished it with a Moorish screen lit with a yellow bulb, big brass fender, a couch and two armchairs, a naughty picture of a nude framed in gilt. Later, in America, he took to wearing conservative suits and to having English meals served in his home. He insisted that his children defer to adults, never to speak until spoken to he asked them to call him 'father' rather than 'dad'; he shunned any real demonstration of affection; he abhorred any change in his habits of living, resisting efforts to change the furniture or to remove the bric-a-brac he had collected over years; he demanded respect for property and privacy, flying into an uncontrollable rage if his edict was broken; he called himself a 'capitalist' with satisfaction; he was careful with his money in small things and invested it shrewdly; he designed his studios as a row of stockbroker Tudor cottages. 'And he always had tea and crumpets with marmalade served every Sunday afternoon at four,' relates his son. 'Tea and crumpets, the symbol of solid English comfort and security, was a little ritual with my father.'[1]

Nevertheless, the class he so ardently wished to leave behind still clung to him. Plutarch's *Lives* and Burton's *Anatomy of Melancholy* were part of the literature he read in public, but by his bedside were pulp detective thrillers. Like the Londoners of the 1890s, he was fascinated by the macabre and the occult and credited himself with extrasensory perception. Murders, suicides, madness, executions and horrifying crimes to children were read about in newspapers and magazines with the same fearful thrill as a child entering a fairground waxworks. He discussed 'sadistic punishments of different races'[2] with his sons in great detail, made up gruesome stories for them and re-enacted some of the more chilling scenes from Dickens. For many years one of his closest friends was a brain surgeon specializing in operations to cure insanity, a man who, strangely enough, eventually committed suicide. Even Chaplin's habit of playing his violin in moods of introspection recalls a hero of the 1890s, Sherlock Holmes.

In his attitude towards sex he likewise showed little evidence that he had completely parted company with the Victorians. Like them he still viewed the spiritual and the physical as being on opposite sides of a great divide. A girl attracted him one way or the other, never both. When he saw Virginia Cherril, who was later to star opposite him in *City Lights*, he recalls that 'her shapely form in a blue bathing suit did not inspire the thought of her playing such a spiritual part as the blind girl'.[3] Faced with that kind of divided viewpoint, one can hardly be taken aback by the way in which he rhapsodizes over his idyllic meanderings with Hetty in one breath and then goes on to describe sleazy dealings with Parisian whores in the next. He is only following the fashion of Victorian man, who, brought up with an impossibly idealistic image of feminine purity, needed the prostitute to relieve himself of the strain. It does not call for too exhaustive a search through Chaplin's films to realize that his heroines lack real sexuality. They can be flirtatious or coy or tomboyish, but never passionate. Anything that smacks of more basic instincts is left to the girl of more dubious credit. If a wholesome girl like Edna Purviance, for instance, is kissed with anything approaching desire, the picture coyly fades out.

The delectable Edna Purviance is seldom kissed with any passion, but in the rare cases when it happens, the act is carefully hidden from the audience's view. These three illustrations come from *The Champion* (Essanay, 1915)

One senses, therefore, that despite the escapades he describes, Chaplin's enjoyment of sex was something less than full-blooded. Perhaps anticipation meant more to him than consummation. Behind the tales he tells of his amours lurks a furtiveness and guilt that ill-becomes his self-designated role of sexual rebel. Someone who could resort to a phrase like 'upper regional domes immensely expansive'[13] in order to avoid saying 'huge breasts' does not invite comparison with D. H. Lawrence. On the contrary, his sexual attitudes might well have sprung from the class that would have reviled Lawrence but simpered at a dirty seaside postcard. There is nothing unconventional but certainly something disappointing about a world-famous man who, having been persuaded to visit Bali merely because he was told that the women there went about naked to the waist, proceeded to nudge

Chaplin looks at this lightly clad prop-room statue in the same coy way as he does his leading lady.

Illustration from *His New Job* (Essanay, 1915)

his brother like a goggle-eyed schoolboy whenever he passed a band of them walking by the roadside. In the light of that particular adventure it seems astonishing that only a few years later he was to be labelled a dangerous subverter of public morals. Indeed, the most shocking example he can put forward as proof of his moral daring is when he advised Mary Pickford and Douglas Fairbanks not to marry but to live together and 'get it out of their systems' – somewhat unexceptionable wisdom, it may be supposed, for the Hollywood of that time.

Since he maintains that sex is not the 'most important element in the complexity of behaviour', we are left wondering which of Chaplin's drives could have taken precedence over sex, or, more accurately, have goaded him the most. In terms of sheer weight, the verdict must be given to fear of ridicule, for nearly two thirds of his autobiography concerns his frantic efforts to avoid loss of face. The account reads like a medieval quest in which Chaplin, armed with a bristling *Roget's Thesaurus* and a crushing *Webster's Dictionary*, takes on the champions of Literature, Science and Politics in Europe and America to win the hand of a fair lady named Recognition. No one who runs through it can fail to be made aware of the enormous chip he carries regarding his lack of formal education. When nearly thirteen he could barely read or write and had to be taught his stage parts parrot-fashion by his brother. Yet thirty-one years later the same person could proudly pen sentences like, 'Were I addicted to cacoethes scribendi I should go into pages of rhetorical rapture extolling the beauties of Vienna. Therefore I shall spare you all too suffering readers any conscious pleonasms on my part.'[14]

The impetus that gave rise to his pleonasms was not in the least virtuous. 'I wanted to know,' he confesses, 'not for the love of knowledge but as a defence against the world's contempt for the ignorant.'[15] Alas, like many others whose perspicacity did not match their ambition, he mistook the shadow for the substance and concentrated on words rather than ideas. They were the obvious insignia that divided him from the distinguished and they were more easy to manage than a daunting backlog of reading. With the nimbleness of a jackdaw he began to pounce on any brilliant aphorism a Great Mind dropped in his path and was sent hurrying to a dictionary whenever a new word sailed into his ken. A few discerning listeners could see through his apparent easy familiarity with abstract phrases; Anthony Asquith likened him to an undergraduate at a literary society. What is truly puzzling is how so many of the intelligentsia seemed to have taken his pronouncements quite seriously. Perhaps they were too polite to say otherwise. He himself comments on an elevated conversation with Lloyd George that, 'In spite of his interest I could not help noticing a stifled yawn';[16] yet there seems to be no record of someone actually telling him to stop making an ass of himself.

In this respect Chaplin's remarkable gift for mimicry stood him in good stead. He could take two or three basic facts about a subject of which he knew virtually nothing, and by reproducing the style of a man of letters, with its rhythms and cadences and its tacit assumption of a whole world of shared knowledge it would be impolite to call into question, he was able to persuade people who did not know him too closely that they were hearing the fruits of many years' extensive reading. The game was a risky one and Chaplin always felt himself balanced on a knife edge. 'My father is egocentric,' explains his son, 'but only those closest to him realize on how sensitive a base that egocentricity rests. A word, a gesture, can deflate him . . .'[17]

Unfortunately, the more he was taken up by the intelligentsia the more he imagined himself on trial. The challenge was too great for him to ignore and his way of life began to change. Gone were the days when he could wander with 'the boys' down to a prize fight or a baseball game or a cheap, friendly restaurant. Elegant soirées with guests like Rachmaninov and Einstein graced his imposing Hollywood mansion and gave him the opportunity of playing his new role of a charming, warm host. Yet he could never have been entirely satisfied. Once he had discovered that 'men of eminence, when I came close to them, were as deficient in their way as the rest of us',[18] the triumph must have worn thin, for it is in the nature of a devouring ego to despise what it has finally conquered, and Chaplin was no exception. His writings are full of references to the 'so-called upper classes' – once, of course, he had been accepted by them.

Having, then, ascended a mountain only to find the view disappointing, he had to look round for other heights to vanquish. The answer was straightforward enough, although accompanied by some irritating complications. The industry he was working in was new, mysterious and influential, and most of its practioners still regarded themselves as students. Gradually it was gaining acceptance as a respectable art form, and already D. W. Griffith had demonstrated its potential. Moreover, Chaplin's own films were being sanctified by several serious newspapers and gobbled up at exclusive literary parties. For a person who could profess that at one time 'the word "art" had never entered my head or my vocabulary',[19] it must have all been very gratifying. What better course than to run with the tide, to succeed where he needed most, to be accounted just as thoughtful, original, knowledgeable in his own field as H. G. Wells or George Bernard Shaw were in theirs? Once decided upon, the change was quickly made. From having entered the film industry simply as a no-nonsense journeyman who looked upon his work as a means of earning money (although with a great amount of professional pride), Chaplin evolved into the artist and theoretician, a new convert to the old nineteenth-century cult which believed creativity to be the only true nobility. Words like poetic, romantic, beautiful, exquisite and artistic tripped lightly off his tongue and much was made of the agonies of creative gestation. By 1916 he could declare: 'The Elizabethan style of humour, this crude form of farce and slapstick comedy that I employed in my work, was due entirely to my early environment and I am now trying to steer clear from this sort of humour and adapt myself to a more subtle and finer shade of acting.'[20] In one sentence he had repudiated all the precious music-hall training which had helped him to become the superb performer he was.

There were snags, however. Unlike a writer or a painter, a film director cannot be entirely responsible for his creation. Many skills are involved and several key people can influence the course of a film from its inception to its final form. Chaplin came as near as anyone to being absolute master, but not nearly enough to satisfy his ambition. It must have irked him considerably that whereas the intellectual giants he hoped to emulate could work exclusively to their own standards, he had to rely on the craftsmanship and artistry of technicians to pull him through. The reliance, too, was considerable. His knowledge of screen technique was rudimentary and bound by an innate conservatism. He also had a natural antipathy towards technical matters. The men who helped him were expert and resourceful, they had been in the film industry since its beginnings and were keenly alive to all its innovations. How was it possible for him to square his new role of absolute overlord with their inconvenient obtrusiveness? Once again the answer was straightforward. He simply ignored their existence. In not one of his writings or public utterances does he acknowledge the extent of the contributions made by his technicians. In fact, they are fortunate if their names are mentioned. Even actors, whom Chaplin treated with more patience and understanding than his technicians, could fall foul of his ego. Woe betide any of them who told him bluntly that he was wrong, or advised him what to do, or who threatened to rock his throne – as witness Ben Turpin having to leave Essanay when he had received almost as much acclaim in the trade press as his director. The

Turpin's individualism presented Chaplin with a challenge in *His New Job* (Essanay, 1915). The two men were not friends, and after Chaplin's next film, *A Night Out* (Essanay, 1915), Turpin left to become a successful Keystone star. He is to be seen in the four-reel version of *Charlie Chaplin's Burlesque on Carmen* (Essanay, 1916), though the sub-plot in which he appears was not filmed until after Chaplin left the company

battery of men who surrounded him and plied him with ideas invariably had those ideas rejected, only to find that they had not been entirely forgotten. 'I let them sink into my mind,' blithely replied Chaplin to an interviewer's question, '. . . and later I find them valuable.'[21] The directors who assisted him were similarly treated.

'Chaplin always used a director, because he couldn't be out in front of the camera and back of it at the same time,' revealed Carter de Haven, 'but he never gave them credit.'[22]

When he was given more time to make his pictures, he indulged in literally miles of film, repeating again and again the smallest action, bamboozling his actors by never demonstrating the same point in the same way twice in succession. His cameraman was always on tenter-hooks because of Chaplin's annoying habit of performing on a spot which was different from the one originally chosen, or because he would suddenly add new business that needed to be photographed at once before it was forgotten. His editor was given scenes which did not cut together because of mistakes in continuity. But when things went patently wrong, 'He'd look for some excuse, something wrong, somebody else to be at fault.'[23]

Yet, ironically enough, in spite of, or perhaps because of, the time spent, the money involved and the amount of reshooting necessary, Chaplin was accorded the reputation of a perfectionist. The word, however, is misleading. It carries all sorts of overtones of artistic integrity and quality which have somehow moved in without the permission of the owner. By itself it tells us nothing of the nature of what is being perfected. One could presumably call Hitler a per-fectionist if one went solely by the number of times he rehearsed his speeches or the attention he gave to the design of his officers' uniforms – though most people would probably hesitate to do so. What the word has come to be confused with is struggle – for an idea, a vision, an interpretation which we instinctively realize is an ideal. Yet, an artist who works with enviable facility, who hardly has to change a note, or a word or a brush-stroke, need be no less a perfectionist than one who has constantly to reject what he has done. Indeed, he may have a clearer idea of the perfection towards which he is reaching. Even one who does have to pass through a long and painful process of elimin-ating what he considers to be second best, does so in the knowledge, albeit intuitive and dimly perceived, of what is first best. And he must care deeply about it, so deeply that he is willing to pursue it even when others do not recognize that what he has achieved is better than what he might have settled for.

Chaplin had no such crusade. His aim was to please and his audience was his arbiter. When, at his previews, they laughed, the gag was kept; when they failed to respond, it was thrown out. If he went over his scenes again and again, or cut off a few inches of film here and there, if he built a set before he had any idea of what the film was to be about and then tore it down once the filming had begun, it was not at the imperative demand of a vision of perfection which imposed its own will upon his, but simply because he had no such vision. Thomas Burke remarked, 'There is nothing, I think, that he deeply cares about,'[24] and that cannot be a description of a perfectionist. In his battle for a place alongside his famous admirers, Chaplin had forgotten one important thing. They had something to say which they vividly believed in. He had his ambition and his hunger for success, but without the belief his perfectionism could and often did degenerate into mere fussiness over trivia. Many years later Gloria Swanson was watching him rehearse Marlon Brando in a scene: 'You see why actors find him difficult,' she whispered. 'This is a simple scene, and he's making much ado about nothing.'[25]

In one way at least Chaplin did preserve an important part of his early life. No matter how far he went into the role of philosopher, he could never get away from the influence of London. It always exerted its fascination over him, and, as Thomas Burke claimed, in every one of his films there is something, a street, a park, a shop, which he immediately recognized as belonging to Lambeth or Walworth. As Burke and Chaplin shared almost identical backgrounds, one can believe him. Certainly on the trips Chaplin paid to his native city he made a point of revisiting all the remembered spots of his childhood and youth. The obvious reaction is to wonder why – with so many bitter memories of poverty and neglect – he bothered to do so at all. No one would have thought it unnatural if he had ignored south London altogether, and concentrated on drowning his past in the Savoy Hotel. On the contrary, many accused him of being morbid for climbing the stairs to the room where his mother went insane or walking alone through the corridors of the orphanage.

Thomas Burke advised him to take a more active interest in what was going on around him so as to leave no time to worry about whether he was happy or not. 'No-o-o,' replied Chaplin dubiously, 'but it's not easy for everybody to be interested all the time. And any-way, I like being morbid. It does me good. I thrive on it.'[26]

Was he really being morbid, or was he trying to find something that he had lost? At one time in his life his horizons were fairly clearly circumscribed: a solid, middle-class home, a brilliant career in the music hall, a stable family life. Within that circumference he could move freely and at ease, never having to question who he was, or why he was, or whither he was going. The unlimited freedom that suddenly burst upon him in America must have caused a sensation like weight-lessness when all the movements of limbs and body that one has taken for granted no longer produce the same effects. Whatever he said was greeted like a proclamation, whatever he had desired was granted to him in overflowing, whatever his ambitions had sought now seemed laughably modest. It was no longer a simple matter of realizing his limitations by the amount of obstacles he bumped against; there were no more obstacles. Not many people can withstand adulation, and Chaplin, who had no particular liking for humanity anyway, was amazed and confused by it all. At least in London his life had been comparatively simple. The money he earned was within the compass of his imagination, many decisions were made for him, he had none of the burdens of a big star and his aims were limited. 'Top of the bill in a West End music hall. That was all I wanted. That was the limit – the maddest dream – the most hopeless goal. To be a Chirgwin or Robey or Albert Chevalier.'[27]

More important still is what London had come to represent. Apart from the nostalgia which everyone feels for a place where some of the most momentous happenings of one's life have occurred, Chaplin needed London as an actor needs his script. It had given him a role, his very first, and one moreover which he did not have to choose for himself. The years which he spent there were the most impressionable of his life. They had thrust him into situations which called for responses utterly intuitive and basic. When he was on the point of starvation, he had to find work; when his mother went mad, he had to protect his own sanity; when he went to the workhouse, he had to deal with people for whom the niceties of society no longer existed; when he went to the orphanage, he was forced to mix with children who would resent any hint of an upstart in their midst. He had to put up with loneliness, hit back at scorn, use his wits against violence and harden himself against shame. Later, in palmier days, working the Northern circuits, he could explore himself a little more, but even then he was still up against hard-bitten performers and had to contend with the dreary round of cheerless boarding houses, the seeping melancholy of industrial towns and some of the roughest music halls in the country. In those years of childhood and youth, when character should be searching for form, he was stamped with it.

Hollywood did not call for the same responses. His distinguished new companions required less of instinct and more of intellect. The one area where he could call upon the old, ingrained reflexes was in the film studio, but even that was being transformed by his yearnings for more respectable recognition. Outside of the studio his London self was suppressed so successfully that Thomas Burke could say that 'he is in manners, speech and attitude, American'.[28] Yet it must have been there, all the same, forcing its way to the surface, released at last when the taste of steak-and-kidney pie brought such a rush of memories that he left for England twenty-four hours later.

Once arrived he was in no-man's-land. On one side, Hollywood shot her flares into the sky and lit up unclaimed vistas; on the other, the mute, dark streets of his childhood waited to engulf him once again. Hollywood required his talent, not his soul; London required his soul, not his talent. There could be no compromise, one or the other had to be abandoned.

Nearly eight years had passed since he had left England. He could now look at it as a man who was world-famous and a millionaire. Presumably he could have settled here if he had wished, built his own studios, employed his own crew, could have used the actual locations that he re-created in his films. But he didn't. The man who had incorporated so much of London's cockney spirit in his work fled the city almost as soon as he arrived. Success in America had changed his perspective. What he now saw did not hold the same power over him that it once had held. The early years of struggle and bitterness could be seen in a softer light, a kindlier one – he even called the streets 'gentle' – and it was possible to become reconciled to them. And that he could never afford to do. London had to remain the same for him, the same frustrations, the same sadness, the same helplessness, even the same people roaming the streets of his youth. It had to remain unchanged in his imagination, otherwise the main source for his creative drive would have left him. To experience the city as he needed to experience it he had to live away from it, or the dream would have gradually succumbed to the reality.

## 5. References

1. Charles Chaplin, *My Autobiography*, London: The Bodley Head, 1964.
2. ibid.
3. Charles Chaplin Jnr, N. Rau and M. Rau, *My Father, Charlie Chaplin*, London: Longmans, Green, 1960.
4. Chaplin, *My Autobiography*, op. cit.
5. *Woman's Home Companion*, September 1933.
6. Thomas Burke, *City of Encounters*, London: Constable, 1932.
7. ibid.
8. Chaplin, *My Autobiography*, op. cit.
9. ibid.
10. Chaplin Jnr, *My Father*, op. cit.
11. ibid.
12. Chaplin, *My Autobiography*, op. cit.
13. ibid.
14. *Woman's Home Companion*, September 1933.
15. Chaplin, *My Autobiography*, op. cit.
16. *Woman's Home Companion*, September 1933.
17. Chaplin Jnr, *My Father*, op. cit.
18. Chaplin, *My Autobiography*, op. cit.
19. ibid.
20. *Motion Picture Magazine*, January 1916.
21. *New York Tribune*, 10 December 1917.
22. *Silent Picture*, Summer 1972.
23. R. E. Totheroh in *Film Culture*, Spring 1972.
24. Burke, *City of Encounters*, op. cit.
25. Kevin Brownlow, *The Parade's Gone By . . .*, London: Secker & Warburg, 1968.
26. Burke, *City of Encounters*, op. cit.
27. ibid.
28. ibid.

# Six

'Our term "slap-stick" derives from Harlequin's bat, a stick made of two limber pieces of wood bound at the handle which made a very loud racket when applied vigorously to an exposed rump' – David Madden in *Film Quarterly* (Fall, 1968)

Whether Chaplin ever saw a Keystone production before he began his first picture for Sennett is open to conjecture; he certainly makes no mention of it. But he would have found it difficult to deny all knowledge of the name, for by the time he arrived, having already taken in two lengthy tours of the United States, the Keystone creations were well on the way to becoming the most powerful influence on the American comedy market. The year 1913 had brought the studios a net profit of some like $3,000 a week, of which a third went to Mack Sennett, and his company could boast of a production list containing over a hundred titles. But nothing could be further from the truth than to deduce from these figures that Keystone was a streamlined operation. Sennett was no orderly and disciplined businessman and his method of

Mack Sennett, the originator of the 'Keystone Kops', was Chaplin's first employer in his film career. His first film for Sennett at Keystone was *Making a Living*, released in the United States on 2 February 1914. That year Sennett produced three one-reelers and one two-reeler every week

making films would have shaken the faith of any but the most unbounded of optimists. His partners, Kessel and Baumann, on the other
hand, were cast in a different mould. Strictly organized and scrupulously ledger-ridden, they sat in New York and controlled the weekly
expenditure and pay accounts, organized the number of prints to be
distributed every week and decided on the publicity and advertising
for each comedy. Sennett did not like them and distrusted their book-
keeping. The boom in Keystone's fortunes and the fact that he wished
to experiment with two-reeler films needing more careful planning
induced him to seek a way of reorganizing the studios as well as
reducing the power of Kessel and Baumann. For this task he chose
George Stout, a business manager who had been with Universal and
Carl Laemmle. With Stout's arrival in the spring of 1913, the Keystone
studios began to lose their haphazard, free-and-easy appeal and to
assume the lineaments of a responsible adult. Ten new departments
were created, each with its own head; credit with local merchants was
established; new stages were commissioned from an architect, perhaps
for the first time in the film industry. More and more of the adminis-
tration was taken out of Sennett's hands, leaving him free to concen-
trate on production.

The interior of the Keystone studio
as it appeared in *A Film Johnnie*,
Chaplin's fifth film for Sennett. Note
the natural lighting and the general
pandemonium. Chaplin must have
found it difficult to act in a situation
in which his colleagues were not
required to remain silent

In that field, at least, the Keystone tradition remained almost untouched. 'The same mixture as before,' the public intimated, and Sennett saw no good reason to thwart their wishes. A graduate of the Biograph studios and the tuition of D. W. Griffith, he had acquired no mean technical ability and knew how to sustain pace and rhythm and to build up to a climax. Uneducated and mercenary, brutal when drunk and boorish when sober, he nevertheless possessed one quality common to all successful businessmen selling a popular product: his taste was at the same level as that of his audience. When Sennett laughed there was a very good chance that millions of others would laugh also. Obviously he was not infallible, but he had the good sense to assemble round him a comedy team of unprecedented talent which more than made up for his mistakes. But one must never forget that the speeded-up action, the deluge of visual jokes and the hairbreadth flirtation with lunacy which form the hallmarks of the typical Keystone comedy were largely the progeny of his vision.

Into this incandescent world Chaplin was suddenly catapulted. His first film *Making a Living* was dogged by a battle of wills between him and his director, Henry (Pathé) Lehrman. Viewing it today, one is made painfully aware of how ill at ease and unready for screen acting

Posed photograph, probably taken to promote the new Chaplin image which first appeared in *Kid Auto Races at Venice (California)*. Chaplin's second film, a split-reel made on location, was the first time he used the costume that was to make him famous. With him in the photograph are cameraman Frank D. Williams and director Henry 'Pathé' Lehrman

Chaplin really was. There is never a moment's repose. Chaplin is continuously, irritatingly on the move, fidgeting, grimacing, fiddling with his clothing. Astonishingly enough, except for the famous hop round corners, every future gesture of the 'Little Fellow' is there, but ill-defined and disordered. Yet the *Moving Picture World* saw this very

Chaplin kisses the newspaper proprietor's bald head in *Making a Living*, his first film, and repeats the same idea in *The Adventurer* (Mutual, 1917), sixty films later. Eric Campbell, the ex-D'Oyly Carte Opera Company singer, who was killed in a car accident soon after, is the victim in the second film

weakness as part of the role and praised Chaplin accordingly: 'The clever player who takes the role of the nervy and very nifty sharper in this picture is a comedian of the first water, who acts like one of Nature's own naturals.'[1] The film, nevertheless, was not a great success, and Sennett began to wonder if his judgement had betrayed him. It is interesting, however, from another point of view. In his editing, imaginative use of the camera (two tracking shots are particularly excellent) and construction, Lehrman showed that he was a very competent, if not a talented, film maker. The tales of his insensitivity towards Chaplin's genius, of his jealously, his obstinacy and his mediocrity, are most probably the interpretations of those who could not understand that had Lehrman allowed Chaplin to do exactly as he wished, the film would have taken much longer to complete and might have ended disastrously. Lehrman's detractors tend to forget, perhaps, that although Chaplin was familiar with many of the Keystone comedy ideas, he was out of his depth when it came to filming them.

Henry Lehrman films Chaplin's dash through the Los Angeles streets from the back platform of a moving tram in *Making a Living*

This might seem surprising when one considers that in an important way Karno, Chaplin's mentor, and Sennett were very much alike. They both worked from the barest of story outlines, leaving much to chance and improvisation. The script for *Mumming Birds*, for example, the most famous of Karno's sketches and the one in which Chaplin starred for several years, can be typed on half a sheet of foolscap paper. The most important details of action and characterization are covered by 'Business to be arranged'. Nevertheless, the differences between the two men were for Chaplin of more significance than the similarities. It was not by chance that Karno's troupes were celebrated for their impeccable timing and control; having once been a circus acrobat, their employer still appreciated the value of exhaustive and careful rehearsing. Chaplin himself states that six months was the shortest period of working together necessary before an ensemble might lose the label of 'scratch crowd'. Sennett would have considered that a ruinous indulgence. One or two days was the time required for shooting a picture; a director was allowed 1,000 feet of film and no more; the actor's rehearsal time was cut to a minimum. No wonder Chaplin was despondent. Above all he needed time, the opportunity to work relentlessly and repeatedly at a routine.

Even though the theatre had given him that chance, the cost was high. Once a Karno routine was set it need never change, but could go on indefinitely, preserved orally from generation to generation like a Norse saga. *Mumming Birds* ran for over thirty-five years, and was only beaten by *Charlie's Aunt*. Most of the actors who played in a sketch called *Wow-Wows*, loosely based on *Mumming Birds*, were bored to tears by its banality, Chaplin among them. By comparison, the film world must have appeared a veritable cauldron of ideas and activity. Even before he had set eyes on Sennett, Chaplin was scheming to film Karno's sketches. He was also accustomed to witnessing some of Karno's best actors deserting for Hollywood. Wary as his inborn caution might have made him of joining the exodus, he could not have been entirely sanguine about remaining behind. Though fighting gamefully, music hall was expiring. Film, on the contrary, was sweeping the country, and it must have entered Chaplin's head that sooner or later, as one of Karno's leading comedians, he was going to be approached with an offer to become a screen actor. For years most of his biographers accepted the story that the idea was anathema to him, and that when the offer finally did come he agreed to it only after much painful soul-searching. His autobiography helped to dispel that assumption, but it is difficult to understand why it arose in the first place. From having experienced films as part of the staple music-hall programme, he would have realized that they held no real terrors for him. Far from being an alien form of entertainment, the basic situations of screen comedy were not markedly different from what he had been doing for years.

This was especially true of the Keystone brand and, as already indicated, his apparent unhappiness at the beginning could not have been simply the result of seeing the type of humour that was being filmed. No popular entertainment is conceived in a vacuum, and Sennett owed his inspiration to ageless patterns of comedy, the same

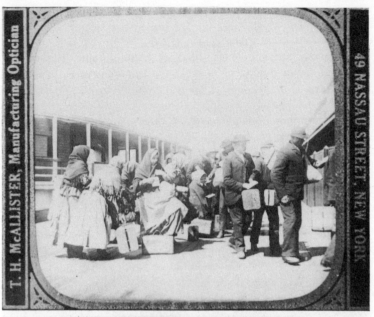

This lantern slide, showing immigrants waiting to pass through Immigration Control around the turn of the century in New York, is not dissimilar to the still from *The Immigrant* (Mutual, 1917), in which film Chaplin recounts what were probably his own experiences of arrival in the land of promise in 1910. Edna Purviance (centre), and (right) Kitty Bradbury, her mother in the film

kind that appeared in the English music hall and pantomime. Authority, pomposity, conventional morality, humbug and wealth were targets shared by all three. The figures that were ridiculed were virtually identical. Perhaps comedy is limited in the number of situations and characters it can exploit; this might explain why every generation seems to throw up the same archetypal figures to caricature, no matter what their country of origin. To the millions of immigrants who helped swell the population of the United States from 50 million in 1880 to 75 million in 1900, the characters that appeared in Sennett's productions must have been comfortingly familiar, otherwise they would have rejected them. It needed a considerable suspension of disbelief to accept these outrageous caricatures who capered and grimaced and chased each other among real backgrounds like warehouses, parks, wharves and streets – a juxtaposition which, one might assume, would have made them appear even more implausible. But to the newly arrived immigrant they were neither outlandish nor incomprehensible, merely variations on the fables, myths, traditions and legends with which popular comedy has always surrounded itself.

Henry Lehrman chases Chaplin after he steals his photograph of a car going over a cliff. *Making a Living* was shot on location in the streets of Los Angeles. The Keystone Studios were actually at Glendale, California

Needless to say, Sennett himself was utterly unaware of his respectable antecedents, and it was only after critics had pointed out the true origins of his comedy that he remembered the rationale that went behind it. 'They reduced convention, dogma, stuffed shirts, and Authority to nonsense, and then blossomed into pandemonium,' he says of the burlesque and vaudeville comedians among whom he had once worked. 'I especially enjoyed the reduction of Authority to absurdity, the notion that sex could be funny, and the bold insults that were hurled at pretension.'[2] His enjoyment was undoubtedly less cerebral and more instinctive, which was exactly the way his future audiences were to react, but whatever his initial response, he was shrewdly to exploit that humour in all his films. Much of his inspiration, it is true, came from early French films which revelled in trick photography, primitive jokes, extravagant buffoonery and wild chases, but it was the spirit of the Commedia dell' Arte, of vaudeville and burlesque, which informed all his work and gave it its dynamism.

Vaudeville takes its name from Vaux de Vire, two valleys in Normandy by the River Vire. In the fifteenth century, Olivier Basselin, a miller of the district, composed a series of cider-drinking songs which spread throughout France. These, in turn, inspired a form of popular, unsophisticated balladry which then evolved into songs accompanied by spoken dialogue, which nowadays we would call 'patter'. Towards the end of the seventeenth century, at the larger French fairs, such as Saint-Germain, these songs were much in vogue and the programme in which they featured became known as 'vaudeville'. It was probably first used professionally in the United States when, in the 1881 Christmas edition of the *Dramatic Mirror*, Tony Pastor claimed that his New York variety theatre was 'the first speciality and vaudeville theater of America, catering to polite tastes, aiming to amuse, and fully up to current times and topics'. Its content differed hardly a jot from variety, the same artistes could appear in both, but whereas vaudeveille took to the road and toured the length and breadth of the United States variety remained static.

This could prove a distinct advantage in that it fostered a local identity. A variety theatre would draw talent from the district in which it stood, and its proprietor would book old turns or encourage new ones with the complete assurance of one who knew intimately the taste of his clients. Theatres differed from district to district. At one extreme was the Bowery beer-hall which drew the roughneck and the drunk, and at the other was the famous Koster and Bial's music hall where the elegant and exalted could wile away their time in the cork room, the walls of which were studded with vintage champagne corks, each bearing the signature of the purchaser. In an age which seemed to happily combine an inward raciness with an outward piety, all the variety houses shared one characteristic – an entrenched disapproval of what was considered to be unseemly language. Even a hall like

Harry Hill's, which was notorious for its sporting crowd, brawls and Bowery prostitutes, would ban a performer for the slightest breach of propriety. Yet there was much that was suggestive and coarse. The Prospect Garden Music Hall, an attempt at an English hall, purveyed a fair amount of this kind of entertainment. One can imagine the rather bizarre effect produced as, watched by the beaming German family who ran the hall, the English serio-comic George Beauchamps stood on a stage in the midst of the tables and delivered a song called 'Oysters' with lines like:

> 'They're all very fine and large,
> They're soft and fat and prime . . .'

making it quite clear by his gestures what he really had in mind. There was also Lottie Gilson, an American Marie Lloyd, to whom, evidently, everything was allowed. One of her favourite ballads was of a girl with a rip in her bathing suit who had asked Little Willie to make repairs with a safety pin. With a face of innocence and a wicked overemphasis she sang:

> 'For he knew just what to do,
> Just the same as me or you;
> He had to kneel to pin it,
> And it took him a whole minute,
> *For he knew just what to do.*'

Before the turn of the century, just over a quarter of the songs in American variety were English. There were man-about-town songs, naughty songs and bass and baritone songs with splendid titles like 'Larboard Watch' and 'Twixt Love and Duty'. Music-hall character acting also influenced its American counterpart and carried over its respect for the truth. For example, an equal to Gus Elen or Chevalier in his minute observation was Frank Bush, a comedian of the 1890s. Though light-haired and German, he managed to hit off to perfection an old East Side Jew.

With his long, tapering black beard, his spectacles, and Prince Albert coat, he looked, talked, and acted the part flawlessly. It was studied mimicry. On Grand Street, near Pitt, there was a pawnbroker called Old Man Nelson. This was the character that Frank Bush studied. He watched him wait on customers day after day for years.[3]

The 1890s also saw the heyday of another English import – clog dancing – and contests were held up and down the country. The two British champions, Wheatley and Trainer, arrived to do battle with Johnny Bickart, an American champion, on the stage of a theatre called, appropriately enough, 'The London'. To make the job of listening to every tap much easier, the judges had elected to sit under the stage, even though the theatre was regarded as unsafe. When the contest was over, they emerged covered in dust and almost asphyxiated. But by far the most sensational import of the 1890s was the Can-Can, which burst upon Koster and Bial's and then, in a series of migrations to Coney Island and the Bowery, degenerated into the shimmy, the scantily dressed revue and finally the 'strip' show.

As the new century took over, farce, musical comedy and vaudeville took hold of the American public. It became the era of the matinée idol and the circuit owner, one nourishing the other. Stripped of its liquor, variety gave way to vaudeville. The new industry, for such it was, guaranteed six weeks' work for an artist and undertook to provide a balanced entertainment which would keep the same high quality wherever it was performed. Gone were the days of the enterprising manager who stood or fell by his own judgement; entire programmes were now dictated from a head office. Wide-flung circuits carried new songs and acts to an audience that might never have heard or seen them otherwise. Bigger and more ornate theatres were raised – places like the Hippodrome, which could take a parade of animals including elephants and house a monster swimming tank for Annette Kellerman and her bathing beauties. By 1909 there were

Annette Kellermann and her serving maids in *A Daughter of the Gods* (Fox, 1916). This film, almost as spectacular as *Intolerance*, was shown mainly in legitimate theatres at $2 a ticket

1,200 vaudeville acts touring the country, over 1,000 dramatic and musical shows, more than a hundred burlesque troupes and dozens of circuses. Inspired by the waves of imimgrants from Europe, vaudeville comedians launched into dialect turns – German, Irish, Jewish. The famous 'My Brudda Sylvest' swept through every vaudeville audience in the country. The Italians replied with the 'Mariuch' series – 'Mariuch Makea-de-Hootch-a-ma-Cooch, Mariuch she Take da Steamboat.'

The restraints and prudery of a few years before when the New York Public Library had decided that Shaw's *Man and Superman* should be put in the reserved section for special readers – thus bringing down the wrath of the author and his remark that America was nothing but a 'provincial place' – that era was passing. America began to take a pride in its naughtiness. As Edward Marks, a prolific lyric writer, wrote:

> Those early-century years in American life were the era of the potted palm, a plant representing the ultimate in splendour and Continental wickedness. No private house was complete without tiger rugs, a den panelled with fake Oriental weapons, and Schreyer's paintings of Arabs detonating their flintlocks from the saddles of shiny grey stallions.[4]

Chaplin poses as Count Chloride de Lime in an attempt to win the hand of the delectable Edna in *The Jitney Elopement* (Essanay, 1915). In this frame Chaplin gingerly enters Edna's palatial residence, complete with its obligatory potted palm

Roof gardens became the rage, and it was in one of them, the 'Jardin de Paris' on the roof of the New York Theater, that the new freedom found its most sophisticated expression. In 1907 a chorus of beautiful girls in bathing costumes, all decorously wearing stockings, launched the first of Mr Zeigfeld's *Follies*. Not content with that sensation he topped it by incorporating in the show the 'Dance of the Seven Veils' from Richard Strauss's *Salome*, which had been the biggest theatrical scandal of the year, even inviting the censure of the Metropolitan Opera House in which it had appeared. 'In the production repudiated by the directors of the Metropolitan Opera House,

'... a line of pretty girls in bathing costumes would immediately ensure the success of anything they appeared in ...' Mack Sennett's famous Bathing Beauties

Mme Fremstad was clothed in seven veils,' drily reported one critic. 'She had the best of Mlle Dazie by six, and even hardened first-nighters gasped.' The next year the *Follies* appeared again, and the same critic, evidently present with the same audience, declared, 'The Taxicab Girls in scanty costumes, headlights and signs of "To Hire" on their red tin flags, brought out a real gasp . . .' The *Follies*, of course, became an institution, and once and for all popularized the notion that a line of pretty girls in bathing costumes would immediately ensure the success of anything they appeared in – a fact Mack Sennett was to exploit later.

Pure stripping, if one can use the expression, had gone on since the 1890s when buxom performers had reduced themselves to flesh-coloured tights. The 'Girl in Blue', a notorious slack-wire and trapeze artiste of the time, had gone so far as to throw her fancy garters at gentlemen in the audience. However, stripping was confined mainly to burlesque, and this strange American hybrid had a history which reached back even further than vaudeville.

The technique of placing a person of authority or fame in a situation where his behaviour must appear incongruous was, to all intents and purposes, first exploited by Aristophanes. Sketches of

Vesta Tilley's famous song, 'Burlington Bertie', tells the story of a man-about-town, a swell, who has a private income and is a good touch or catch for the girl who wants to make a good marriage. Chaplin often

played a swell when he was with the Karno troupe, and adopted this pose for his first Keystone film, *Making a Living* (1914)

Socrates scanning the heavens from a balloon, or of Cleon, a dema-gogue, portrayed as a sausage seller, were considered extraordinarily bold for the Athens of that time. Oddities and affectations in dress or behaviour were thrown into relief and made to appear ridiculous by this method. It exposed bombast, empty rhetoric, sham virtues and blatant hypocrisy. The laughter it provoked, unlike satire, was not malicious in that it liberated rather than wounded. By making 'gods speak like common men and common men like gods', burlesque served to remind society in the pleasantest of ways that its laws, customs and traditions were not immutable but open to change if the will to do so existed. In the course of time the message was blunted, but the method still remained popular. The habit spread through Europe. Chaucer was fond of using it. Early in the sixteenth century, Italy gave it its name from the *Opera burlesche* of Berni. In France, under Louis XIV, travesties of the epics of antiquity became the height of fashion and led, much later, to the *opéra-bouffe* of Offenbach. Burlesque was introduced to England by J. R. Planché, who produced his first work for Drury Lane in 1818. Twelve years later, he collaborated with Madame Vestris, who appeared in 'travestie', and wrote for her a piece named *Olympic Revels* in which she played Pandora. For the next sixty years, 'classical mythology, history, the plays of Shakespeare, opera and current drama were explored continually by men of letters who were masters of the decasyllabic couplet and the popular art of punning'.[6]

Some of the most accomplished and wittiest writers of the age were engaged to write burlesques, men like W. S. Gilbert, George Augustus Sala and Henry J. Byron. Nevertheless, in spite of its honourable literary connections, middle-class Victorians still frowned upon burlesque. From its earliest days, one of its main attractions had been the sight of women displaying their limbs in scanty men's attire, and of men impersonating loud, vulgar women – vulgar, at least, by the standards of those days. John Hollingshead, who took over the Old Gaiety and brought to it some of the most sparkling of burlesque, was apt to describe himself in his golden days as a 'licensed dealer in legs,

Female impersonators were common in the music hall, and Chaplin himself made a convincing woman. Here we see him in *A Busy Day* (Keystone, 1914) and in *A Woman* (Essanay, 1915). The former film, a split-reel, was only rediscovered in the 1970s; and the latter, in which a man makes approaches to a man dressed as a girl, must have seemed quite a daring theme for 1915. In some countries it was actually banned by the censors

short skirts, French adaptations, Shakespeare, Taste and the Musical Glasses', revealing a realistic sense of priorities and a certain kinship with Mack Sennett. He it was who, drawing upon music-hall talent for his species of 'burlesque-drama', influenced Augustus Harris to

Chaplin upstages Eric Campbell in *The Cure* (Mutual, 1917). This scene is very reminiscent of a Victorian melodrama. Eric is the villain and Chaplin the hero

introduce into his Christmas pantomimes at Drury Lane burlesque and music-hall artistes of the calibre of Vesta Tilley, Herbert Cambell and, of course, the inimitable Dan Leno. By 1882, a critic and theatre historian could bewail the fact that 'pantomime is dead, and that burlesque of the most deteriorated type has usurped its place'.[6]

Perhaps because of its associations with briefly clad women, burlesque in the United States developed into a predominantly 'girlie' show. Its roots were respectable enough for all that. Gilbert and Sullivan were great favourites for burlesque, and none of the celebrities of the day was spared its treatment. A typical and very successful sketch was one on Paderewski entitled 'Paddy Whisky' in which the performer played a trick piano with his toes and nose. Women minstrel shows which toured the country would also feature parodies on politicians at the hustings, a part of the programme which was retained when the shows went out of fashion and were converted to burlesque troupes. Thus burlesque, in spite of its transformation, managed to hold on to some of its traditions. Unavoidably, with the increasing foreign population and the vast differences between city and city or town and town, burlesque began to pander to the lowest common denominator. Parody degenerated into crude slapstick and naughtiness into coarseness. One of its worst aspects was its increasing cruelty. Grotesque, misshapen creatures were used as the butts of low comedians, and even thrown about the stage, in much the same way as was happening in the circus. Neither was the cruelty necessarily confined to the lower classes. One theatre in New York held an 'amateur night' once a week in which excruciatingly bad artistes, having been encouraged in their ambition by the management, were introduced to an audience of brokers and men-about-town who mocked the performance unmercifully and threw rotten vegetables on to the stage. Undoubtedly some of the victims were less naïve than their audience imagined. A particularly bad actor by the name of 'Count Joannes', whose speciality was a ludicrous Hamlet or Romeo, pocketed $1,500 a week as a result of amateur nights; and an equally inept act called the 'Cherry Sisters' could earn as much as $1,100.

In keeping with its custom of pillorying the social vices, burlesque still hit out at hypocrisy, pomposity, wealth and so on, but the fun, now bereft of its original purpose, had become a mere exercise in violence. It became the fashion to view all forms of authority as a natural enemy, regardless of their worth – an outcome, perhaps, of the oppression and poverty much of the population had undergone in Europe. The most common form of authority was the police force, and the Keystone Kops were a surrealist extension of what Sennett had seen in burlesque. But the policeman as a figure of scorn goes back

A frame enlargement from *His Regular Job* (originally known as the *Thief Catcher*), a Mack Sennett Keystone comedy starring Ford Sterling and Mack Swain, showing the Keystone Kops rushing to the scene of the crime.

much further. One has only to think of Dogberry, the constable in *Much Ado About Nothing*, to guess that his roots might well begin in antiquity.

English pantomime subscribed to the tradition. As early as 1725, John Rich, the first great pantomimist, devised *Harlequin Sorcerer, with the Loves of Pluto and Prosperpine*, in which the mischievous Harlequin is chased by a village constable who 'at last catches him; he tumbles down 'midst his guards, and slips away from 'em'.[7]

Once the 'Peelers' had been formed in 1829, they materialized as symbols of fierce satire and as butts of the clown. They were spared nothing. Sadler's Wells introduced a sketch called 'A Preparatory School for the New Police' into one of its Christmas pantomimes in which the constabulary were shown up as thieves, pickpockets and bullies. After that it became obligatory for every harlequinade to include at least one policeman at odds with the clown or Harlequin. In a description that could almost be a scenario for a Sennett comedy, George Augustus Sala, writing in the 1870s, pictures a typical pantomime scene in which:

The policeman was presented as a comic figure; the butt of much crude humour, in places of entertainment.

Outside their walls, he was respected and often feared

shopkeepers are tripped up, old ladies are pushed, young girls romped with, babies sat upon or crammed into pillar boxes; there were vegetables, lobsters, codfish, plaster casts and legs of mutton flung about the stage. There is a general row; the police make their appearance, and are duly bonneted and trampled upon . . . and the scene closes.

The music-hall policeman, on the other hand, was not subjected to the same sharp satire. A slow-moving and in most cases bovine character, he was not corrupt but cowardly, derelict in his duty when

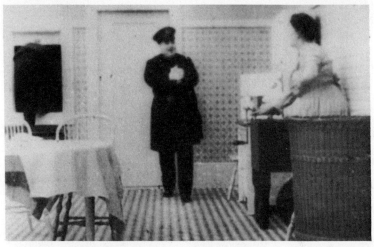

Chaplin was true to tradition and pictured policemen in his films as naïve and stupid. In this shot from *The Count* (Mutual, 1916), Frank J.

Coleman pays a visit to Eva Thatcher's kitchen. His intentions are dishonourable

he left his beat to gossip with the cook or the maid in the basement of a rich family's house:

> After goose and rabbit pie,
> Down area steps a stealer,
> Courting cookies on the sly
> Goes Peter Potts the Peeler.

Numerous songs about him graced the halls. Little Tich rendered 'I'm an Inspector of the Metropolitan Police' and Albert Chevalier ambled his way through 'The Village Constable', a dimwitted example of the breed. The policeman became an institution fairly early on, a state of affairs whimsically summed up by Seymour Hicks when he

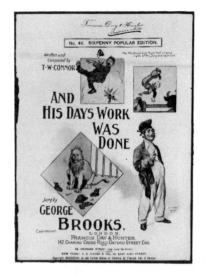

In 1903, the motor car and the policeman were both figures of fun. In T. W. Connor's song 'And His Day's Work Was Done', they come face to face, as they were to do so often in the early days of the cinema

remarked to a young admirer: 'You will recognize, my boy, the first sign of old age; it is when you go out into the streets of London and realize for the first time how young the policemen look.'

Harlequin has been mentioned as being linked to the policeman in pantomime; he himself was a product of possibly the greatest example of comic improvisation Europe has ever seen. Evolved during the sixteenth century, Commedia dell' Arte has managed to influence every branch of popular comedy up to the present day. As most of Sennett's actors were enlisted from a wide cross-section of popular entertainment, it would be surprising if, through them, Commedia had not crept into the Keystone fold.

The stock characters of the Commedia have reappeared in various guises through the centuries. There were three sets of them – professionals, servants and lovers – who interacted with each other in highly complicated and perplexing love intrigues.

Among the professionals, Pantaloon, an elderly, grasping merchant, was usually a widower with a lively coquettish daughter, but sometimes was cuckolded by a wife much younger than himself. He wore a reddish-brown half-mask with a hooked nose on which were perched spectacles, and he grew a pointed beard. His fate was to pursue an elusive dream of passionate *amours*, only to be constantly outwitted by the other characters in the play. His close friend was the Doctor, either an astrologer, a lawyer or a physician. Pedantic in style, but a bogus academic in reality, the Doctor had a habit of throwing facts together into a stream of gibberish or of quoting lines of inaccurate and doggerel Latin. His half-mask was black and included a stubby, pointed beard. The Captain, the last of the professionals, blustered and bragged about his conquests, both female and military, swaggered about in fine, rich clothes and a plumed hat, but dodged if anyone sneezed, or fled behind cover in the face of a naked threat. His mask was flesh-coloured, with a bristling moustache and a huge nose.

The next group of characters were the *zanni*, or comic servants. Brighella, employed by a rich rake, assisted his master's *amours* but would help anyone for money. Thoroughly unscrupulous, a thug and a thief, he prowled through the Commedia in a sallow mask with a hooked nose and curled, fop-like moustache. But he was a strange, ambivalent character. An expert on the guitar and flute, he could sing pleasingly and dance gracefully, and was capable of moving an audience to tears even in the midst of his villainy. His brother, Pedrolino, was a valet and also the lover of Columbine. An engaging, charming dreamer, sensitive to a fault, he was inclined to be rather simple. When the French took him over he became Pierrot and his simplicity shaded into pathos. He wore no make-up, but his face was covered in white flour, a tradition Chaplin was to exploit when he insisted on flat, white make-up with no highlights or shadows. The eldest of the servants was Pulcinella, who became the English Punch. Aggressive, energetic, with a fierce, outsize hooked nose, he was a grotesque creation. He had a hunched back and a pot belly, and he hopped about like a beady-eyed hen, emitting a 'cheep' at every other pace or so.

The most famous of the *zanni* was Arlecchine or Harlequin. He is the most difficult to depict. Originally a simpleton, gluttonous and forever in love, he was fair game for everyone, being continually kicked or cuffed; yet he remained supple, agile and gay. In time he became more cunning, less ingenuous, but he never completely sloughed off his initial characteristics. Because of this he could react in many different and often contrary ways, exhibiting an elusiveness that gave scholars an eager chance to write reams about him. Simply put, he could be as unpredictable as a child, or as consistent as an adult, utterly at the mercy of his instincts one moment, sweet reasonableness the next. Of all the Commedia characters, he is the one to whom Chaplin is most compared. Lastly, the female counterpart of Harlequin was Columbine, a sparkling, witty and coarse servant of the Inamorata, for whose numerous affairs she acted as go-between. She was also pleasure-loving and promiscuous, entering into casual liaisons with any one of the other characters. In many illustrations showing her and Harlequin together, he is either fondling her bare breasts or thrusting his hand under her skirt.

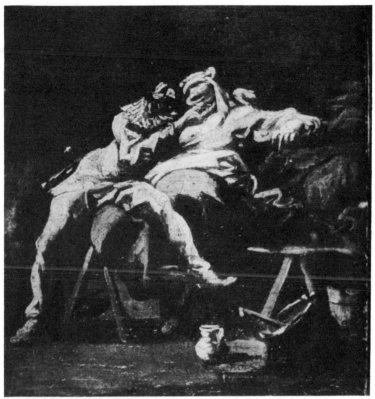

Arlequin

Much Victorian humour derived from the Commedia dell' Arte, which, though formalized, was often vulgar and crude. In these illustrations featuring Harlequin, we see both sides of his character. With his club in his belt and his face masked, he is just a simple clown. But when he drinks with Columbine and cocks his leg over hers (a gesture Chaplin was to imitate many times in his films), he becomes a leering debauchee

Chaplin's routines often involved touching his fellow actors, another characteristic of the Commedia dell' Arte. In this shot from *The Property Man* (Keystone, 1914), Chaplin looks somewhat lecherously at Alice Davenport's pretty leg. In *The Floorwalker* (Mutual, 1916), Chaplin's hand inadvertently comes into contact with the customer's foot

In contrast to the lusty and open sexuality of the servants, the last of the groups, the lovers, declared their passion in chaste, euphuistic prose, bursting with classical references. Their characterization was much less defined than the others, and they were merely a counterpoint or a pivot for the buffoonery.

For all their limitations, the characters of the Commedia managed to generate a vast number of scenarios. Something like 800 have come down to us, while many others have been lost. The love intrigues became so preposterously involved that scrolls bearing a short summary of the plot were let down at the back of the stage for the audience to read. Having been given the barest outline of their own part by the manager, the actors worked out the points at which to enter or leave, then walked on to the stage to perform a virtual improvisation for the next two hours or so. Into this fabric the salient points of the story were dextrously and amusingly woven.

There was very little material that the actors could not use, everything was grist to their mill – local stories and scandals, the dialect of the district they happened to be playing in, tricks of speech or oddities of dress they had learned from petty officials, topical news, current jokes. Their audiences were not onlookers but participants. They had their favourite stars and stories. They were the final judges as to what was kept or rejected. If a piece of improvised business worked well with them, it was used next time; if it failed to please, it was never seen again.

As the Commedia evolved, its store of jokes, dialogue and business increased. The actors began to learn many of the successful speeches and jokes by heart. Business which had once been improvised became a stock-in-trade to be used when and where the occasion allowed. The skill of the actor became not only a matter of inventiveness but of seizing the right moment to launch into a set speech, of picking up a stray cue that could spark off a train of familiar business. He had to play within a team, to efface himself when necessary, to take the centre of the stage when the action was flagging, to be alive to the timing, the idiosyncracies and the intentions of his fellows. Above all, he had to exercise his sense of proportion.

This was particularly true when it came to introducing the *lazzi* into the action. Literally meaning 'ribbon', this wound its way in and out of the plot and was the Commedia's most powerful catalyst. In an age in which science was just beginning to reduce everything to order, the *lazzi* was a paen of praise to chaos. One might, perhaps, describe it as the mouse giving birth to the mountain. It might start with a slap across the rump. The recipient retaliates with a poke in the ribs. A fierce argument develops which, like a widening vortex, sucks in more and more members of the cast until the stage is covered with a wild tableau of acrobatics. Many *lazzi* could also be set in motion by one of the buffoons breaking into a lover's scene and parodying their formal, aery dialogue in dumbshow. But whatever the original cause of the *lazzi*, its effect and emphasis had to be nicely judged or it would have toppled the play into pointless violence. No *lazzi* therefore was

The art of mime required considerable athletic prowess, and Chaplin's apprenticeship with Karno stood him in good stead for scenes like this. Here he makes a successful attack on Bud Jamison in *The Champion* (Essanay, 1915)

ever left to chance. Though inserted in a spontaneous way, its actual working out was carefully planned. Falls, somersaults, leaps, hand-springs and the like were part of its vocabulary, a basic requirement for any Commedia artist. And he had to execute them cleanly. Most of the stages on which he acted were narrow trestles erected in the piazzas of small towns, allowing for no margin of error. Visentini, one of the greatest of Harlequins, could turn a somersault with a glass of wine in his hand and not spill a drop.

With such emphasis placed on physical dexterity, it was natural that the body be regarded as an extra prop, to be used like any other. The backside came in for most attention. As its owner turned or walked backwards or bowed, or as he bent to look at something, it was

This painting in the Louvre by du Jardin, entitled 'Les Charlatans italiens', shows a group of Commedia players performing their traditional entertainment on a makeshift portable stage deep in the countryside

Although billed as a 'laughable farce' and featuring a would-be Blondin, this street entertainment in Britain in the second half of the nineteenth century still has strong links with the Commedia performance above

Chaplin was so adept at performing feats which required considerable agility that they did not even interfere with his characterizations. Charlie's remarkable dance with Miss Moneybags (Edna Purviance) is the high point of *The Count* (Mutual, 1916), an accurate and biting parody on life at the top. In *The Rink* (Mutual, 1916), Charlie's performance on skates has a balletic quality worthy of a dedicated professional

Many comedians exploited the comic potential of the posterior, and Chaplin was no exception. Indeed, he himself and many of his characters are often forced to adopt somewhat unnatural poses to precipitate the inevitable comic business. Bud Jamison, Edna's admirer in *In the Park* (Essanay, 1915), strikes an inviting pose which Chaplin cannot ignore. In *The Floorwalker* (Mutual, 1916), Chaplin treats Albert Austin's backside with measured respect while the shop inspector, Tom Nelson, looks on. Finally, in *Triple Trouble* (Essanay, eventually released 1918), Billy Armstrong desperately tries to prevent Chaplin's backside from sticking up in the air while he is sleeping

knocked, kicked, pricked by a sword, scorched by a hot surface or patted approvingly. Skull, nose and ears were tapped, tweaked and pulled. Toes were stamped upon, backs slapped too heartily. Beards were twisted and teeth extracted with huge fearsome pincers. Bare breasts and buttocks were stroked and pinched. False, monstrous phalli were paraded about like regimental colours and bowels were evacuated in uninhibited mime.

Other props were part of the location in which a scene was set, and, indeed, many locations were chosen because of the props they provided. The apothecary's shop was a common setting, furnishing the Doctor with a 'stock *lazzi* prop – the enormous enema syringe; drawings show posteriors bared to receive the enema, which sometimes splashes an old woman's face'.[8] Objects could turn against their owner with surprising ferocity as if they possessed a life of their own, and in coping with them the Commedia artist showed a delightful ingenuity. A recalcritrant prop could either be used as a weapon against an opponent or pressed into some useful function for which it was never designed. A stool that refused to be sat upon could suddenly develop into a helmet to ward off the blows of Harlequin's stick.

This painting, showing a Commedia performance, demonstrates a preoccupation with the behind:

'. . . the enema, which sometimes splashes an old woman's face'

Paradoxically, however, the most fertile source of inspiration sprang from the Commedia's most difficult limitation, the mask. By covering two thirds of the face, not only did it prevent the actor from using one of his most vital means of expression, but it also reduced the resonance of the voice, producing a curiously muted effect. As dialogue was of major importance in the Commedia, the actors were obliged to seek ways of emphasizing their words to make their meaning clear and their dramatic effect more telling, while at the same time conveying the emotion covered by the mask. They solved the problem by using large and unequivocal gestures. Thus mime became an integral part of the Commedia. The body and limbs developed into sensitive instruments almost separate from the actor. He might talk of 'playing the

Like the Commedia player, Chaplin was a master at expressing feelings with every part of his body. In *The Tramp* (Essanay, 1915), Chaplin's back tells us all we need to know about his feeling of despair; and in *Those Love Pangs* (Essanay, 1914), Charlie manages to flirt in the cinema with Cecile Arnold (right) and Vivian Edwards by using only his legs

back' or 'playing the head'. A whole range of poses was invented, each one telling the audience something different about the character. Particular gestures or acrobatics became associated with certain roles, and players could spend years perfecting a gesture or stance unique to them. Scaramouche loved to box a man's ears with his feet; Harlequin became identified with a flat-footed walk, a special way of wielding his stick and of playing with his hat; Pierrot flapped his arms like a giant bird.

To enhance even further the differences in their roles, the actors wore distinctive clothes. The lovers were dressed in the same style as the more fashionable members of the audience, whereas the *zanni* sported ill-fitting or motley-coloured costumes. Pantaloon shuffled about in Turkish slippers with turned-up toes; Pulcinella wore white linen trousers which bellied out from his legs like balloons; Brighella crept about in gleaming braid; Harlequin leapt and spun in heelless shoes. The costumes of women were not as sharply defined, mainly because they were not as crucial to the drama as the men. They were picked for their beauty rather than their acting skill. Some of them were also ballerinas – a great attraction of the Commedia where dance and music were an integral part of the drama and not merely performed in the interlude. In a performance that could go on for three hours, they provided a welcome relief.

In spite of its length and its limitations, Commedia managed to retain a firm hold on the popular imagination. Its golden period lasted for about a hundred years and brought a youthful and fresh alternative to the sterile religious and academic drama that was the fashion in Italy. Southern Italy produced a more boisterous Commedia, one which tended to submerge character in a deluge of *lazzi* and horse-play; northern Italy cultivated a more restrained playing that was subtle and witty, allowing characterization to provide the springboard for the action. Both eventually degenerated into tasteless farce, employing hunchbacks and dwarfs for crude and easy laughs and going in for more and more sensational acrobatics. By about 1800 it was dead. But its influence continued: in pantomime, in the circus, in some of the music-hall sketches. Over a hundred years after its death, silent film comedy brought back some of its spirit. Critics found shades of Pantaloon in John Bunny and W. C. Fields, the Doctor in Oliver Hardy, the Captain in Ford Sterling and Wallace Beery – even in the ubiquitous cop on the beat. Langdon and Harold Lloyd revived memories of Pierrot, as, on occasions, did Chaplin. Mabel Normand, a perfect foil for any comic, merged into the boyish Columbine. Perhaps it is not too fanciful to see in the meeting of Chaplin and Sennett the old rivalry between the two forms of Commedia: on one hand, the elegant, fastidious Harlequin orchestrating the chaos around him; and on the other, the worried, extrovert Commedia manager whose experience had convinced him that the way to make an audience laugh was with a stream of continuous *lazzi*.

## 6. References

1. *Moving Picture World*, 17 February 1914.
2. Mack Sennett and Cameron Shipp, *King of Comedy*, London: Peter Davies, 1955.
3. Edward Marks, *They All Sang*, New York: Viking Press, 1935.
4. ibid.
5. Ernest Short, *Fifty Years of Vaudeville*, London: Eyre & Spottiswoode, 1946.
6. W. Davenport Adams in *The Theatre*, February 1882.
7. *Gentleman's Magazine*, 1752.
8. David Madden in *Film Quarterly*, Fall 1968.

# Seven

'I've often thought of my popularity. I've never been impressed by the magnitude of it. I happen to have the good fortune to work in a medium that has a large circulation' – Charles Chaplin in *Woman's Home Companion*, September 1933

Chaplin had to appear in twelve films before Sennett finally capitulated to the slower, more considered comedy of the Englishman. Only then was he allowed to take over completely the writing and directing of his own work. But the process had been hastened by increasing public recognition. Already with his second film, *Kid Auto Races at Venice*, Chaplin had given a slender hint of his future screen creation, with the result that one alert critic could claim, admittedly after he had seen several subsequent Chaplin films, that on beholding *Kid Auto Races* he had immediately recognized it as being the funniest film he had ever seen. He was also moved to declare that Chaplin 'does things we have never seen done on the screen before'.[1]

To the eyes of a modern viewer, however, there is nothing remarkable about *Kid Auto Races*, even less so when considered against Chaplin's later achievements. It is a diversion rather than a film, almost an attempt at a comic newsreel. The idea – that of a buffoon getting in

Chaplin plays the buffoon on the race track at Venice, California, while the crowd who have come to watch the children's cart races look on. It is probably Frank D. Williams behind the camera in this shot from *Kid Auto Races at Venice* (Keystone, 1914)

the way of a film unit trying to photograph a public event – might have been suggested to Chaplin by a visit he had paid to Jersey several months previously, when he had evidently been much amused by a man making a nuisance of himself in front of a crew trying to film the annual carnival. Another tale relates that there is or was a newsreel in existence showing Chaplin, then a youth in his early teens, pulling faces at the lens of a camera recording a Guards' parade. Whatever its

Staring into the camera was a favourite Chaplin trick. He treats the lens like an audience in *Kid Auto Races at Venice* (Keystone, 1914); and like a viewfinder in *A Film Johnnie* (Keystone, 1914)

source, *Kid Auto Races* has since been hailed by biographers and critics as an event absolutely crucial to his career. Robert Payne, perhaps the most elaborately effusive of Chaplin's admirers, asserts that it 'came like a bolt of lightning'.[2] If so, it fell well out of Chaplin's earshot, for in his autobiography he never gives it so much as a mention.

Its real importance, as far as he was concerned, might have been altogether different and much more immediate. With only one moderately successful film to his credit, he was given the opportunity of a solo performance. True it was to be only part of a reel and thus under five minutes long, but it was a chance that few, if any, of Sennett's actors had been granted in the past. It came through no sudden burst of generosity on the part of Chaplin's employer. He merely needed someone to be funny in a particular place at a particular time, and Chaplin happened to be free. He probably also wished to give his new comedian a second audition, just to quieten his doubts about the man.

Chaplin must have realized the importance of the occasion. The idea was simple and he could develop it. There was no need to rely on the timing of a partner. The camera set-ups were of the most basic kind, cutting technicalities down to the minimum. It was obvious that even with Lehrman directing him, he was going to be able to impose his own style and pace on the picture. It was a golden opportunity to find out whether what he considered right for himself was also right for the screen.

In the event, the discovery was a happy one. Sennett was impressed; the Englishman made him laugh, even though his pace was much slower than the customary Keystone hysteria. Of course, the tough, determined purveyor of slapstick had no idea that what had walked on to the children's racetrack was an embryonic 'Little Fellow', and in all probability neither had Chaplin. His own accounts of how he felt when, for the first time, he donned the motley assortment of garments for the film, have varied as often as he has related them. Sometimes they were planned, sometimes pure chance, sometimes a mixture of the two. On the principle, therefore, that an acorn grows into an oak and not the other way round, it would seem safe to assume that Chaplin's new clothes did not burst upon him as a divine revelation, but were merely a practical way of looking funny. The film itself seems to bear this out. If the legend is true that the 'Little Fellow' materialized

Although Chaplin's costume changed little from the one he got together for *Kid Auto Races at Venice* (Keystone, 1914), his walk and movements were then much stiffer than in later films

complete once his clothes had been assembled, then it cannot be Chaplin who appears in *Kid Auto Races*. The walk is stiff-legged, quite unlike the 'Little Fellow's' floppy waddle, the bowler hat is never doffed, the cane never springs to life, the moustache is never twiddled or perched disdainfully over pursed lips, the hand is never cupped over a grin or a laugh, the knees are never hugged in sudden joy or embarrassment, no one is tripped, kicked from behind or hooked on the handle of the cane. And the grimaces thrust at the camera are more in the style of Ford Sterling, whom Chaplin was meant to replace. There is something of the 'Little Fellow' there none the less. It is in the silhouette, slightly less exaggerated than it was to become, but altogether as visually clear cut as a cartoon.

In terms of what had gone before this was a great advance, and goes part of the way in explaining Chaplin's almost unparalleled ability to attract the public's notice from the very beginning. An artist would have been hard put to it to sum up early screen clowns like André Deed or Charles Prince by as sparse a means as a bamboo cane, a shabby bowler and a cracked pair of boots, a set of symbols which in only a short time were instantly to summon up Chaplin to millions of people. One might have accomplished the same kind of thing in the music hall where, in the early years of this century, comedians wore clothes for comic effect. George Robey's parabolic eyebrows, pork-pie hat and slender cane, Little Tich's outrageous boots, Mark Sheridan's conical trousers – all of these could have been made into swift and

Chaplin's success depended partly on the fact that he was recognizable even if he was only partly visible. In this shot from *Those Love Pangs* (Keystone, 1914), the Chaplin silhouette in the distance attracts more attention than Chester Conklin's coversation with Cecile Arnold in the foreground. Likewise there is no doubt who is behind the door in the shot from *The Vagabond* (Mutual, 1916)

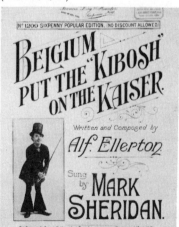

Music-hall artistes appreciated the importance of distinctive costume, as did the Commedia players. Here George Robey (right) and W. S. Lester show they are meant to be young boys by the length of their trouser legs; and Mark Sheridan creates a lasting impression with his bizarre flared trousers

familiar caricatures. But the screen clowns went too far. Theirs was an excess of paint and costume pushed to the point where everything is so grotesque that nothing is outstanding. Had they simplified their dress but retained a certain eccentricity, they might well have arrived at a sharper characterization. In this connection, one might mention an extremely powerful and instructive exercise for actors. If from a selection of half-masks an actor picks one which fits him comfortably and then turns towards a full-length mirror and sees how it looks on him, the effect is startling. Within a few seconds another spirit seems to possess him. All sorts of things begin to suggest themselves – a voice, a stance, a walk, body movements, gestures. In the course of time this first impression can be built upon, in much the same way as Chaplin was to construct the 'Little Fellow'. Though there is no indication that anything as potent happened to him the moment he tried on his costume, there is little doubt that it was the costume that sparked off the character, not the reverse. This is not to deny that the indications were already there. It has been noted before that in his first film he showed many of the characteristics of the 'Little Fellow', though they were unfocused, as it were. What the costume provided was a matrix, something to bind the elements together.

Whether the early clowns could have taken advantage of a discovery such as Chaplin's is doubtful. French comedy, which dominated the screen's early years, left little margin in which to develop the idiosyncrasies, mannerisms and attitudes of a distinct personality. Though attempts were made to break through the convention of purely physical humour, they were not particularly radical. André Deed, the first of the clowns to try to shatter the mould, was extraordinarily popular and internationally famous. He was known, according to the fashion of the time, under a multiplicity of names – 'Cretinetti' for the Italians, 'Grebouille' for the French, 'Foolshead' for the English, 'Teribio' for the Spanish, 'Glupishkin' for the Russians – but this did not mean that his personality was just as variegated. He possessed but one notable characteristic which he brought to bear on every situation, a breath-taking mindlessness. He was capable of pick-axing his way through the wall of a police station rather than using the door; he could wreck every stick of furniture in his home while pursuing a sudden interest in gymnastics; he could burn down his house by bringing in a candle-lit Christmas tree; he would use a candle and a sheet of paper to light a cigarette. Full of the photographic tricks pioneered by Méliès, Deed's films possess technical ability and polish, but the central character never travels beyond the confines of the action, never exists in spite of it.

All the early clowns were similarly trammelled. Not being granted the opportunity to explore all the possibilities dormant in a situation, they were not given time to explore themselves. This ran contrary to the trend in popular stage entertainment. For several years past the great comedians were the ones who showed an audience how they dealt with reality and not how reality dealt with them. As this demanded time to reflect and experiment, they evolved their acts over many years. Pathé and Gaumont, the two protagonists in the film comedy field, could ill-afford such a luxury. With a schedule of two or three films a week each clown was expected to summon up an instant character which would elicit an instant and uncomplicated response. Hence the procession of fat men, thin men, tiny men, henpecked men, timid men, boastful men and lecherous men who passed across the silent-comedy screen in its first few years. The more wonder it is that Chaplin, in spite of having to play in thirty-five films in his first year, could manage to develop such a subtle and complex persona.

Part of the reason for this as well as for the success of the 'Little Fellow' must lie indirectly with the attitude of the early film-makers towards speech. At the turn of the century in France, theatrical comedy was in the hands of authors like Caillavet and Robert de Flers who produced a succession of light, sophisticated satires on academic, political and society life; or it flourished in the poetical plays of Edmond Rostand, whose *Cyrano de Bergerac* and *L'Aiglon* relied almost entirely on a brilliant manipulation of language. It was thus inconceivable for the early film producers, steeped in theatrical tradition as they were, to consider the possibility of a comedy based on character or wit which did not contain dialogue. There seemed no alternative but to turn to low comedy for their raw material. The first screen clowns were therefore recruited from vaudeville or variety, burlesque and the circus, places where speech took second place to slapstick and where the main qualifications for work seems to have been a talent for tumbling and the stamina to perform for long hours at fever-pitch. Helped with a liberal amount of trick photography, the clowns dutifully transferred their skill to the cinema, complete with the make-up, costume and gestures appropriate to a small figure on a large stage rather than a large figure on a small screen. Nevertheless they did not have it all their own way, despite their enormous popularity. Many discerning film-goers soon resented a type of humour 'at the mercy of mere mechanical devices, of waterhose, and dust-sheets and interminable masses of sticky dough, and ice-cream that covers the actor's face as with whiskers'.[3]

Inexplicably, no one seems to have recalled a famous tradition of acting which, though speechless, was as eloquent as any the stage had seen. Not a hundred years before, in the Théâtre Funambules in the

Boulevard du Temple, the art of pure mime had been brought to perfection by one of its greatest exponents, Jean-Gaspard Deburau. As Pierrot, he had begun his career in almost the same way as Chaplin, by adopting a new set of clothes. Instead of the ruffles traditional to the role, he changed to a loose white cotton coat and trousers, white shoes and a tight black skull-cap. From being a comparatively minor figure, almost subservient to Harlequin, Pierrot was transformed into the

Marcel Carné's *Les Enfants du Paradis* (France, 1944) starred Jean-Louis Barrault as the famous mime, Jean-Gaspard Deburau, who was born in Bohemia in 1796. In these two scenes from the film, which was carefully researched, Barrault shows Deburau's acting technique. According to Robert Payne in *The*

*Great Charlie*, the 'beauty of Deburau's acting lay . . . in his nonchalance, his simple joy in defeat, his sudden rages, the little scamperings of the feet which announced his momentary triumph'. This description is equally applicable to Chaplin

pivot of the play. Deburau's emotional range was awe-inspiring. A moment of unrestrained bedlam could be quickly turned into the most delicate pathos by the faintest of smiles on his white, death-like face. He was stillness itself. His movements were restrained, limber and hypnotic. Surrounded on stage by violence, he yet preserved a centre of detachment. Hundreds deserted the classical theatres for a glimpse of him, and in his career of some sixteen years, the greatest writers of the day paid him homage. But it was the ordinary people who really adored him, the rough, turbulent crowd who came from the district in which his theatre was set. No strangers to the extremes of passion and violence, they could readily identify themselves with Deburau's eerie changes of mood.

Their equivalent, many years later, was to form the bulk of the followers of silent film comedy. All that was missing was a Deburau, a man who could make the silent screen speak through mime. When he did come along, there was no overnight revolution. Max Linder, née Gabriel Levielle, had to work in the usual way of Pathé clowns

Chaplin had great respect for the French comedian Max Linder, and may well have seen his films in Britain or the United States, or in France, where he appeared briefly with the Karno troupe at the Folies Bergères. Although always immaculately dressed, Linder also relied on bizarre situations for humour, such as this one, where he is trapped by a simple hook

until he developed a style of comedy acting which has influenced every major screen comedian up to the present day. That he was allowed to do so was mainly due to his incredible efficiency. Where Chaplin would have spent hours puzzling over gags, photographing them again and again until he was satisfied, Linder used to rehearse briskly from a well-prepared script, then shoot the scene once without a mistake. His output was staggering. In nine years with Pathé he made over 400 films, not all of them masterpieces, but most of them redeemed by his brilliance. His versatility was unbounded and his ideas seemingly inexhaustible. He played a cab driver, a skier, a skater, a hunter, a balloonist, a waiter, a yachtsman, a juggler – and a deluge of others.

As Chaplin told of his own arrival in America in *The Immigrant*, so Linder did likewise in *Max Linder Goes to America* (*Max Comes Across*, 1917). Geo. K. Spoor imported Linder as a replacement for Chaplin after he left Essanay for Mutual. However, Linder was not successful and only made three films in the United States on his first visit. He played the real man about town and audiences were unable to identify with him as they were with Chaplin. In many other respects, however, the comedians' techniques were very similar

The common denominator was his character: that of a stylish, impeccable chaser of women – married or single – a cause of havoc wherever he went, a smooth, elegant boulvardier on the alert for a quick conquest or a quick touch, but above all a self-imagined diminished aristocrat having to stoop to make a living by whatever means available. Chaplin's debt to him is considerable. He once sent a photograph of himself to Linder inscribed – 'To the one and only Max, "the Professor", from his disciple, Charles Chaplin.' And the characters they played were strangely alike, even though the 'Little Fellow' aped his supposed betters while Linder's dandy had to put up with his supposed inferiors. They both used a cane as a fifth limb, they both sported a black moustache and fancy waistcoat, they were both small and dapper, they were both superb mimics.

But whereas Chaplin's miming was an integral part of English popular entertainment, Linder's miming set him apart from his contemporaries. Burlesque and circus-trained comics could not compete with this varied, expressive way of projecting character. A rapier had been substituted for a cudgel. The paradox was, or seemed to be, that this new actor who proved himself an ideal screen comedian had trained originally for the theatre, performing in farces or satires which were the very antithesis of silent film comedy. However, Linder had been coached by Charles Le Borgy, secretary to the Comédie Française, a theatre which includes mime in its curriculum. Indeed, it would be surprising if this were not so, considering that Molière, its founder, was heavily influenced by the Commedia dell'Arte. One has only to think of the stylization of a typical Comédie Française production to realize how close to pure mime it does come. Linder most probably received a thorough grounding in mime from Le Borgy, and was then able to adapt it for the screen.

His success was international. 'In the theatre I could hope to be known only in France,' he once said. 'But now these absurd films were chasing themselves all over the world, bringing hundreds of letters from places I had never heard of, and would probably never see.'[4] The urbane, spruce figure was copied again and again. Just before 1914 he was earning £8,000 a year, a truly prodigious sum for those days. In spite of the fact that not a few of the films of this most fastidious of comedians were labelled by the distributors as too strong for those with delicate sensibilities, Linder was the first to inject polish, wit and depth of characterization into film comedy. He extended its range, and in so doing extended its appeal. Sophisticated and knowledgeable audiences were now prepared to approach film comedy with a little more respect.

His message, if one can class his artistry as such, might well have inspired another actor in America to take film comedy equally seriously. John Bunny joined the Vitagraph Company in 1910 when

John Bunny was one of the few well-known and successful comedians in the American cinema before Chaplin. Here he plays Mr Pickwick in an early version of Charles Dickens's *Pickwick Papers*. Bunny also had a background in vaudeville

he was forty-seven, after a successful career in variety, drama and musical comedy. He took part in his first film without a fee, so convinced was he of the future of the industry. Not surprisingly, he too was a master of mime, moving his gargantuan form with great control while a battery of expressions crossed his genial, florid face. Bunny gave to the American public what Linder had given to the French: comedy which was natural and restrained, based in day-to-day reality not in fantasy. They adored him almost from the start. In a poll conducted by *Motion Picture Magazine* in 1912, he was voted the seventh most popular screen artist in the country. After he had found a redoubtable foil in Flora Finch, thin, angular and somewhat prudish, they played together in a vastly successful series of domestic comedies, nicknamed 'Bunnyfinches' by their fans, in which Bunny exploited his range to the full. Much of the humour was generated by the gap

John Bunny and Flora Finch proved a successful team because of their different physical proportions, as illustrated in this still. After Bunny died in 1915, Flora Finch never achieved success on her own

between Bunny's amorous ambitions and the reality of his huge bulk, but there was an innate charm to all his actions, and the figure that came across to the audience was avuncular rather than lecherous. Despite the breakneck speed at which his comedies were made, they revealed an increasing sophistication in plot and technique. Better lighting and dramatic editing were two of the techniques the Bunny films were using at the same time as D. W. Griffith.

But the main reason for his powerful appeal was his breadth of emotion. 'If he is sorrowful there is no room in the hall for any one else's sorrow,' wrote *Pictures and Picturegoer*,[5] and this gives an indication of the underlying seriousness of his portrayal, a fact which did not escape his admirers. Whether playing a costermonger at the Derby or Mr Pickwick, Bunny gave to the role much more dimension than either his predecessors or his contemporaries. His was the first real advance in America from crude slapstick to perceptive, social comedy. Two days after he died on 24 April 1915, the *Manchester Evening*

*Chronicle* carried perhaps the best summing-up of his art: 'When we saw him henpecked and dejected, seated at the breakfast table, withered by the bitter tongue of his formidable spouse, there was something more than laughter in our hearts. There was the least touch of pity, and this was a tribute to the truth and reality of his art.'[8]

Although Bunny's art did not directly influence Chaplin in the way that Linder's had, the American comedian helped to prepare the way for the 'Little Fellow' by demonstrating to the public just how subtle and comprehensive film comedy could be. Linder, of course, had amply proved the same thing, but he was not as popular in America as Bunny, nor as loved. Chaplin, without stepping into Bunny's shoes, was to take advantage of the taste for good, substantial comedy that the American had so carefully built up.

Chaplin was an expert mime, and his training with Karno, who had, as a result of the British law which did not allow actors to speak in dramatic sketches performed in the music hall, become the leading exponent of the art, stood him in good stead when he entered the silent cinema. Here we have two scenes from *A Film Johnnie* (Keystone, 1914). In the first, Chaplin compares his own lean figure with 'Fatty' Arbuckle's substantial paunch; in the second he accepts money from 'Fatty' without acknowledging that it is bribery. The other scenes, from *Mabel's Married Life* (Keystone, 1914), show Chaplin engaging in a very human relationship with the dummy Mabel Normand has placed in her flat

Once again, it was mastery of mime that allowed him to do it. This was Chaplin's supreme gift. No amount of intelligence, perception, emotion and ideas could have taken its place, for without the ability to translate them into gesture and movement, the 'Little Fellow' would have remained a dead letter, a character Chaplin might have dreamed about but never have realized. Just as with Linder, Chaplin's grace of movement and variety of expression made his colleagues appear a gang of bumpkins. Even in the midst of lukewarm praise or decidedly huffy disapproval, the critics had to concede him his artistry. 'Many of his antics belong to buffoonery of the commonplace brand, and most of his pictures are bad enough, surely,' vouchsafed the *New York Dramatic Mirror*. 'But Mr Chaplin comprehends pantomimic expression (most of his confrères do not) which gives a certain value to whatever he does.'[7]

His experience with Karno was invaluable. It had provided him with a vocabulary of mime second to none. Many of Karno's sketches were played to a musical accompaniment, a kind of rhythmic map on which to plant gags and action. Almost inevitably Chaplin's films were to be called rhythmic, his movements balletic. It was said that they would almost suggest their own musical score. On the set he would sometimes use a record or have a musician play a tune that would give him the tempo for a scene, unlike other stars who required music solely for creating the right atmosphere. His medley of kicks and falls was taught to him by Fred Kitchen, a brilliant Karno comedian who was also an expert mime. From him Chaplin learned the famous trick of throwing a cigarette in the air and flicking it away with his foot. Kitchen's outsize boots and idiosyncratic walk – a 'curious shambling

Chaplin often worked the halls with Fred Kitchen, who was a past master at the art of kicking away a match or a cigarette with his heel. Charlie employed the trick many times in his films. Here he is doing it in *Those Love Pangs* (Keystone, 1914)

walk, a cross between a shuffle and a hop'[8] – obviously lodged themselves in Chaplin's mind, to be drawn upon later. Indeed, it was reported later that Kitchen would never play in the United States because he was convinced that the public there would take him for a Chaplin imitator. He was a master of pacing, accumulating laughs by

Fred Kitchen could bring great sensitivity to a sketch, and there seems little doubt that Chaplin learnt a lot from Fred during their time together with Karno

Although one associates the chase and the custard pie with Keystone, Chaplin seldom used these classic gags in his films. There were, however, a few exceptions, like *Behind the Screen* (Mutual, 1916), and this scene from *A Night Out* (Essanay, 1915), where Chaplin is about to cover Leo White's face with a pie

A good comedy situation always exists if a potential victim does not know what is about to happen to him and the audience does. In this shot from *Caught in a Cabaret* (Keystone, 1914), Chaplin is about to hit a troublesome customer over the head with a mallet

a slow gathering of momentum around a central gag, putting into practice Karno's dictum that the best comedy resulted from a fusion of two opposites – a comic who is ignorant of what is about to happen to him, and an audience which has guessed it in advance. When Kitchen died, *The Stage* was anxious to record his natural talent for being able to win the sympathy of an audience, something else his pupil was to carry to Hollywood:

> . . . his gift as a player of sketches, his power to bring tears to the eyes of his audiences, and his robust, clean humour were celebrated throughout the world of music hall . . . He had a remarkable gift for touching his audiences with his depth of pathos, and was said to be one of the few actors able to cry real tears on the stage.[9]

Karno himself drummed into his cast the value of wistfulness, the technique of suddenly switching from comedy to pathos, the trick of wandering about the stage looking lost. A hard and in many ways a bitter man, he had concluded from his own experience that what was basically cruel was also irresistibly funny, a philosophy that Chaplin was to reiterate when he was famous, and which forced him to run the gauntlet of much disapproving criticism.

## 7. References

1. *Cinema*, April 1914.
2. Robert Payne, *The Great Charlie*, London: André Deutsch, 1952.
3. A. N. Vardac, *Stage to Screen*, Harvard University Press, 1949.
4. John Montgomery, *Comedy Films*, London: Allen & Unwin, 1954.
5. *Pictures and Picturegoer*, 15 August 1914.
6. *Manchester Evening Chronicle*, 26 April 1915.
7. *New York Dramatic Mirror*, 7 July 1915.
8. J. P. Gallagher, *Fred Karno, Master of Mirth and Tears*, London: Robert Hale, 1971.
9. *The Stage*, 5 April 1951.

# Eight

This is a very curious world,
So many things are happ'nin';
For all the girls
Wear Pickford curls,
And boys play Charlie Chaplin.

– *Motion Picture Magazine* (May 1916)

The criticism accompanying Chaplin's early films was neither consistent nor particularly well-balanced. The praise he received at the height of his fame was truly remarkable, but like anything taken to extremes, it threatened to topple over at the slightest of public whims. Those who admired him most seemed possessed of a deep ambivalence towards that admiration. They sprang to his defence a little too quickly, a little too vehemently, thus arousing the suspicion that, as well as defending him, they were also protecting themselves. Why this should have been so owes as much to the divisions within the film industry as it does to his own art.

In February 1914 the *Motion Picture Magazine* published the results of a poll conducted among its readers to find out their likes and dislikes. Given the choice between a comedy and a drama, 5,908 people would have preferred to see the drama as against 1,446 who would have preferred the comedy. Yet, in that year, Chaplin was voted top of a 'Popular Players' contest. This gives an indication of the increasing dilemma in which critics found themselves when it came to assessing him. Comedy, slapstick comedy in particular, was still not a worthy subject for serious analysis or discussion. It could only be appreciated by suspending the judgement one reserved for its weightier partners. Its themes were flimsy, vulgar, immoral and too readily appreciated by the masses. There was not necessarily any snobbery in this. It was just that the majority of people still believed that drama could include some comedy whereas comedy could never contain real drama. Many actors and film directors looked upon screen drama as the most powerful way by which to change the world and educate the public, regarding themselves in several instances almost as hierophants of a

When they were first released, most Chaplin comedies supported dramas. The comedy was never treated seriously, even though audiences were often more attracted by the comedy than the main feature. On this bill, *Charlie Chaplin's Burlesque on Carmen* (Essanay, 1916) takes second billing to *The Fall of Babylon*, the historical episode from D. W. Griffith's *Intolerance*, which was released as a separate entity

new order. They viewed their career as a vocation, and were as scrupulously correct in their private lives as they were in their screen roles. George Pearson, a pioneer of the British film industry, probably summed up the hopes and ambitions of all those early idealists when he described the cinema as 'the greatest, the most tremendously powerful force for the bringing about of all that universal brotherhood of the world that mankind has ever known, and only by living for it, giving oneself to it, housing it, seeing it and believing in it, can great things be achieved'.[1]

Beside such noble sentiments, film comedy seemed puny indeed. One was allowed to praise its ingenuity, its high spirits, its speed, its agility, even its sublety, but one could never hope to find worthiness or seriousness. The critics were yet to come across an artist who, in some way, transgressed the frontiers of comedy allotted to him. Chaplin appeared to do just that. Clearly, at the beginning, he had no moral message to deliver, no reforming zeal to express, but there was a quality in him which eventually provoked the kind of intense support or hostility normally reserved for politics, religion and patriotism. What that quality was has been the subject for numerous studies and appears to have meant all things to all men. Nevertheless it is possible to say that after his initial success among those who saw him only as a hilarious comedian, many highly intelligent people were not prepared to forgo the pleasure of seeing him – people who otherwise might never have given a thought to slapstick comedy. Perhaps it was his grace of movement, the beauty of his gestures, the brilliance of his miming which encouraged them to consider him in other terms. There is something vastly satisfying, after all, in the sight of even the humblest of craftsman who is master of his craft. One is tempted to read deeper and more significant meanings into it, especially if the tendency of the age is to feel threatened by a devouring industrialization which seems bent on crushing the individual craftsman – a mood chatacteristic of the early years of this century.

Then, again, it is difficult for thinking people to stop thinking. An intellectual who enjoyed Chaplin found it as impossible to accept him at the comedian's own level as it would be for Prince Charming to keep Cinderella dressed as a scullery maid. And therein lay the intellectual's dilemma: how was he to reconcile his disdain for slapstick with his very real delight at one of its masters? The problem was never solved satisfactorily. Serious critics betrayed a painful inner conflict; between admiration and shame, between hostility and uncertainty. How they wrote about Chaplin was largely determined by how they tried to deal with those conflicts.

At first they were not aware of them. The trade press in 1914 was, in fact, very enthusiastic. 'We do not often indulge in prophecy,' proclaimed the *Exhibitor's Mail*, 'but we do not think we are taking a great risk in prophesying that in six months Chaplin will rank as one of the most popular screen comedians in the world.'[2] Other reviews were almost equally as ebullient, and it would have been considered churlish at the time to predict anything but a smooth, upward glide to success. Then, about half-way through the year, after the press had been more than usually prodigal in its use of epithets like 'side-splitting', 'uproarious' and 'screamingly funny', the *Moving Picture World*, reviewing *The Fatal Mallet*, stated: 'This one-reeler proves that hitting people over the head with bricks and mallets can sometimes be made amusing.'[3]

Whether the review was correct or not is beside the point. What is more interesting is the underlying uncertainty it reveals. The writer is not quite sure if hitting people over the head with bricks and mallets *should* be made amusing; or, to put it another way, whether he should

'. . . hitting people over the head with bricks and mallets can sometimes be made amusing' – extract from the *Moving Picture World*'s review of *The Fatal Mallet* (Keystone, 1914). The shot shows Chaplin with Mack Sennett at his side about to hit Mack

Swain over the head with a mallet. Beside him is Mabel Normand. The other comes from *Police* (Essanay, 1916), just after Chaplin has hit a policeman (Frank J. Coleman) over the head with a club. Hidden behind Chaplin is Wesley Ruggles

laugh at it. Otherwise he would not have used such a strong word as 'proves'. Two months later, the same magazine committed itself still further along similar lines, but in so doing disclosed more fully the confusion of its critic.

There are very few people who don't like these Keystones [he began cautiously]; they are thoroughly vulgar and touch the homely strings of our own vulgarity . . . some of the funniest things in this picture are too vulgar to describe . . . There is some brutality in this picture and we can't help feeling that this is reprehensible. What human being can see an old man kicked in the face and count it fun?[4]

Contemporary critics regarded *The Property Man* (Keystone, 1914) as excessively brutal. This scene, in which Chaplin crushes Charles Bennett under a trunk and then sits on it, seems to bear out the point

Not only was this a clear statement of two aspects of Chaplin's work which were to cause critics much embarrassment over the years – his violence and his vulgarity – but it also illustrated the difficulty they

Since the first films were shown as 'chasers' in the music hall, the early film comedies reflected the kind of humour that music-hall audiences enjoyed. It was often vulgar and cruel, as is obvious in these six scenes. The first shows Chaplin inadvertently pulling off Alice Howell's skirt. In the same film, Charlie throws Fritz Schade out of the door on to Mack Swain, Joseph Swickard and 'Slim' Summerville, who are already lying on the pavement in a heap. In *Mabel at the Wheel* (Keystone, 1914), Chaplin gives Harry McCoy a hefty slap across the face. And in *Twenty Minutes of Love* (Keystone, 1914), Chaplin jumps on Chester Conklin while Minta Durfee watches. It is Charlie's turn to suffer in *His Trysting Place* (Keystone, 1914), when Mabel Normand hits him over the head with an ironing board. Finally, in *The Masquerader* (Keystone, 1914), he kicks Fritz Schade in the stomach

found in trying to come to terms with them. If the Keystones were so popular and the vulgarity they contained so 'homely' – in other words, a perfectly harmless and natural weakness which everyone shares and no one should be ashamed of – why was the writer so loth to describe that vulgarity, especially when it was so funny? The answer must be that he was not sure whether his audience would agree with him and was therefore reluctant to pursue the point further. Brutality, on the other hand, is something one can condemn without fear of reproach. Hence it was a handy way of trying to mollify those readers who might have felt doubtful about their critic's good taste.

For the rest of the year the reviews were mainly favourable, if not wildly enthusiastic. Although the *Moving Picture World* in late September had reservations about *The Rounders*, calling it 'a rough picture for rough people', Chaplin was still a novelty and no one had really taken his measure. When he changed to Essanay in January 1915, he entered the most triumphant year of his career. Month after month he was voted the top male comedian. Chaplin novelties were advertised in film magazines and his figure was displayed on their covers like a black exclamation mark. Postcards were made of him, songs were dedicated to him. Strip cartoonists like Elzie Segal, the inventor of Popeye, related his adventures to an eager public. Essanay ran a huge exploita-

In 1915, Essanay mounted a huge publicity campaign and the fan magazines were soon full of advertisements for trinkets featuring Chaplin, statuettes and toys. These three photographs show a contemporary statuette, a musical toy relying on the persistence of vision, manufactured in France, and the cover of a dance based on Chaplin's well-known walk

tion campaign and poured Chaplin statuettes into department stores and shops, the kind of treatment they had given to Alkali Ike only two years before when an eleven-and-a-half-inch replica of him seated on a hobby-horse had swept America. Chaplin imitators sprang up overnight. Billie Ritchie, who had also been with Karno, did a blatant impersonation of Chaplin down to the smallest detail of costume and gesture, and followed almost every Chaplin film with his own version of the same plot. Two weeks after *Work* had been released, for example, Ritchie replied with *The Curse of Work*. Later he was to claim that Chaplin had copied the 'Little Fellow' from a character he had

Billie Ritchie, who had also been a member of the Karno Company, did a blatant impersonation of Chaplin and appeared in films whose titles were almost identical to Chaplin's own

played in an early Karno farce, but no one took him seriously, least of all several of his former Karno associates. In Columbus, Ohio, a Greek by the name of Steve Duros, who looked the image of Chaplin, dressed up as the 'Little Fellow' and paraded the streets performing somersaults and 'prat-falls'. When he had attracted enough onlookers, he picked himself up and calmly announced to his gaping audience the latest Chaplin releases in the town's cinemas. Jokes began to circulate about a new irritating craze among boys to imitate him, and by June the *Motion Picture Magazine* announced that, 'The Chaplin mustache is spreading – not the mustache, but its popularity.'

Billy West was a better Chaplin impersonator that Ritchie, and it is hard to tell which of these shots actually features Chaplin. In fact, the first comes from Billy West's *Hard*

*Luck* (Emerald Motion Picture); his partner is Ethel Gibs. The other shot shows Chaplin and Edna Purviance in *Work* (Essanay, 1915)

It was in this same year that Chaplin became the subject of more serious attention. He was now, so it was claimed, the most talked-about man in America. One display advertisement in January magnanimously offered exhibitors 'three of the greatest stars the photoplay world has ever seen – the A.B.C. of drama and comedy – Mr G. M. Anderson, Mr Francis X. Bushman, and Mr Charles Chaplin'. *Bioscope*, the English film journal, put out a short but searching analysis of his art (a rarity for publications of those days), in which it was thought that 'perhaps the funniest thing of all is his own complete imperturbability'. Words like 'genius' and 'comic artistry' appeared in letters to film journals. But there was an undercurrent of hostility. Sometimes it took rather subtle forms, as when a reviewer would throw in the word 'average' to describe the type of audience that enjoyed the films. Thus the 'Photoplay Philosopher' wrote about *Tillie's Punctured Romance*:

> This farce was admirably done, perhaps overdone. The familiar Keystone landmarks such as the throwing of pies into people's faces and the kicking and throwing of persons into every ludicrous position conceivable, were prominent throughout, and these items never failed to raise a laugh from the average audience.[5]

Although Sennett thrived on spectacular chase sequences, they were rare in Chaplin comedies. However, the end of *Tillie's Punctured Romance* was certainly in the Keystone tradition: everyone ended up in the water

Occasionally the attacks were less muted, as when Sime Silverman, writing for *Variety*, classed Chaplin's work as 'mussy, messy and dirty', and considered that 'never anything dirtier was placed upon the screen than Chaplin's Tramp'.[6] One might have awarded top marks for Mr Silverman's courage and bottom marks for his good sense had he not ended a particularly excoriating review with 'but since the audiences will laugh there is no real cause for complaint'.[7] One suspects, unfortunately, that he was suffering from the same complaint that afflicted many of his colleagues: lack of genuine conviction in the face of Chaplin's sweeping success. In fairness, however, it has to be added that it must have been extremely difficult to hold on to any contrary opinion while nearly a million votes, clamouring their support for Chaplin as 'Best Male Comedian', were cascading into the offices of the *Motion Picture Magazine*.

At the same time, it must have been impossibly difficult for those who liked Chaplin despite the naggings of their 'good taste' – a phenomenon which, we have seen, was already apparent only a few months after he began with Sennett. One way of dealing with this quandary was to separate Chaplin from his background, to pick up the 'Little Fellow' and dust off the dirt deposited by the demands of a rather sordid occupation. A curious and mystical piece of writing appeared in May in a publication called the *Little Review* which showed what could happen when this attitude was pushed to extremes. It throws more light upon the writer than it does upon Chaplin. When the little figure appears on the screen, relates the writer, it does so

amid the roars and wild elation of idiots, prostitutes, crass, common churls, and empty souls converted into a natural and mutual simplicity. The stuffy, maddening 'bathos' that clings to the mob like a stink is dispelled, wiped off the air. Charlie Chaplin is before them, Charles Chaplin with the wit of a vulgar buffoon and the soul of a world artist ... He is absurd; unmanly; tawdry; cheap; artificial. And yet behind his crudities, his obscenities, his inartistic and outrageous contortions, his 'divinity' shines. He is the Mob-God.[8]

Other articles were not slow to appreciate the message, and throughout the second half of 1915, as the momentum of public acclaim accelerated, they shifted their ground to this novel method of solving their dilemma. 'Mr Chaplin is funny with a funnyness which transcends his dirt and vulgarity,' jubilantly wrote Julian Johnson in *Photoplay*,[9] and his cry must have wrung heartfelt gratitude from the hearts of the uneasy.

Unlike the *Bioscope*, which was content to allow that Chaplin was 'an artist whose genius needs no explanation', American critics were not happy to let things lie inactive. Having accommodated themselves to the more questionable sides of Chaplin's art, even to the point of rationalizing them out of existence, they felt the need to assert themselves. He now had to take guidance from them, to throw off his old clothes and plunge into the clearer, less murky waters of higher comedy. Behind them, they had the support of a fresh campaign for a stricter censorship on marital infidelity, sexual licence and violence.

Towards the end of 1915 the 'Close-Ups' column of *Photoplay* devoted a section to 'The Case of Chaplin', which gave sober voice to the newly found concern for his career.

What is to become of Charlie Chaplin? [began the writer portentously]. Will the little genius of laughter slowly relegate himself to comic history, or will he, changing his medium of expression, pass to higher and more legitimate comedy? He must do one or the other. No one stands still on the highroad of artistic creation. Progress or retrogression is the universal lot, and Chaplin's cycle of dirt and acrobatics is about to run.[10]

The general public was not so sure. Letters to the magazines revealed an increasing tendency for readers to dig their heels in, to resent any intrusion into what they considered a totally innocent way of enjoying themselves. One correspondent, after confessing that he found it excruciatingly funny to see Chaplin take 'a wallop at some unoffending bystander', was at great pains to point out that he was no 'low-brow'. 'I read Schopenhauer, Kant, Ibsen, Tolstoy and Shaw,' he challenged, 'and I enjoy them.'[11] There were a few dissenting voices, a typical example being the lady who was too ashamed to be seen carrying the July issue of *Motion Picture Magazine* with its 'hideous Chaplin cover', but the tone of most of the letters is strangely familiar to a modern reader, stressing as they do the need for realism, for pure entertainment without a message, for a healthy acknowledgement of the seamier side of life.

The critics were not to be put off, however, and in January 1916 there occurred an event which must have given them much heart. This was Chaplin's sudden conversion to respectability, as reported by J. B. Hirsch in the *Motion Picture Magazine*. The National Board of Censorship was pleased to announce, stated Hirsch, that 'the old Charlie Chaplin has seen that the very methods by which his personality achieved success now imperil his unprecedented reputation by alienating a great part of the American public'. The board was even

*A Night in the Show* (Essanay, 1915) was loosely based on *Mumming Birds* (known in the United States as *A Night in an English Music Hall*). In the first shot, Chaplin moves Carrie Clarke Ward's headdress aside so that he can see the stage; Leo White looks on. In the second, Chaplin starts a conversation with May White, a snake charmer

happier to disclose that the practical result would be 'a new fame based on a more delicate art'.

Unhappily, that 'great part of the American public' so desirous of a new, well-trained Chaplin were not to see their earnest wishes fulfilled at once, for the Chaplin film circulating at the beginning of 1916 was *A Night in the Show* – a film so far short of any fresh development in his art as to be comparable to his earliest days with Sennett and even with Karno. The usual hail of hostile adjectives rained down upon it, and even a staunch Chaplin supporter like Julian Johnson of *Photoplay* had to lay his own taste open to attack in the cause of defending it. 'When they showed me this mussy, and at times decidedly unpleasant visual narrative, I punctuated it with ribald shouts,' he confessed. 'I couldn't help roaring.'[12]

Nevertheless, public and producers were still greedy for Chaplin, and in February 1916 he signed a contract with Mutual at a salary of $670,000 a year. The *Tatler*, perhaps in deference to his fame and firmly established wealth, carried an article which named him as the widest-known personage in the world, liking him with distinguished fictional and folk-heroes of the past. It had even asked permission of *Cinegoer* to reproduce a portrait of the star – a magazine, one imagines, whose existence it would normally have ignored.

Yet the fame, and more particularly the Mutual contract, were mixed blessings for Chaplin. A new note crept into the murmurings against him. At first, criticism had confined itself to his work alone; now it began to attack the rewards of that work. This was not a new departure as far as general attitudes went, and Chaplin was not the only one to suffer from it. In March 1915 the 'Photoplay Philosopher', replying to many letters that shared his point of view, affirmed that he could

name dozens of young ladies, who are now getting about thirty-five dollars a week, who, if given Miss Pickford's opportunities, could earn at least 5,000 dollars a year each for their employers and possibly ten times that. Perhaps it's the old story of 'To him that hath shall be given', but put me on record for better salaries for the whole company and only a reasonably small fortune for the 'Star'.[13]

This was an almost direct contradiction to the prevailing American ethic: wealth to those who could manage it, and good luck to them – the kind of sentiment that seems to have prompted one cartoonist to sum up the Chaplin story with the legend: 'From a penniless immigrant stranded in New York – to a small-time comedy acrobat – to the highest paid movie star – is the story of Chaplin's rapid rise to success.'[14]

Perhaps the ethic did not stretch so easily to film-stars because no one really felt that they worked hard enough for their money. Indeed, many of the actors, stricken with the same thought, took unnecessary risks in order to assuage their guilt. It is certain that among all the adulation showered upon them there was a good deal of resentment. Alfred A. Cohn, in the March 1916 edition of *Photoplay*, undertook to lay before the public the true facts of 'What they Really Get – NOW!' The gist of his exposure was that salaries were grossly inflated and that, though producers recognized this, they had no choice but to pay them, forced into it by fierce competition. The highest-paid star, according to Mr Cohn, was Chaplin, and several lines in the report were devoted to the details of Chaplin's earnings with Essanay the previous year. They totalled $175,000. The new Mutual contract, therefore, was nearly four times as much. Unemployment, agitation about tariffs, financial instability, fears about joining the war in Europe and losing vast amounts of money in giving aid to Britain – these were the topics that racked the United States at the time. It was bound to happen that an Englishman who had arrived just over two years before, and was now earning almost the salary of an emperor, would become a target for a great deal of bitterness and envy.

For the moment, however, it fermented under the surface. The Mutual salary was still rumour and not confirmed by the press. Minnie Maddern Fiske, in an impassioned outburst in *Harper's Weekly*,[15] placed Chaplin among the great names in the history of comedy, and thus seemed to prove that intellectuals could never influence public opinion but only follow it. Her panegyric was almost a direct inversion of what his latest critics had been saying. Instead of fending off Chaplin's vulgarity, she flung her arms around it, protesting that without vulgarity no comedy could exist. At the same time as she wrote, a report sent to *Photoplay* seemed to confirm her in her enthusiasm. It arrived from a London badly shaken by the news of the disastrous campaign in the Dardanelles and it told of a Chaplin madness running through the city like an epidemic. Every theatre in the Strand was showing a Chaplin film, some of them dating from early 1914. Every musical revue featured 'at least one actor dressed up to take off Charlie Chaplin. In one revue there was a whole chorus of Chaplins.'[16] *Tillie's Punctured Romance*, originally intended as a vehicle for Marie Dressler, was now advertised as a Chaplin film without mentioning anyone else. In one newspaper bought by the correspondent there were only two instances when the name of a star was thought worth printing: 'Francis X. Bushman in *The Second in Command*, and Charley [*sic*] Chaplin in – well it doesn't say in what. Just a wild exhuberant triumphant, Charley Chaplin! Charley Chaplin! Charley Chaplin!' The power of the name was tremendous, he reported. When Essanay had decreed that Chaplin films could only be obtained by buying the whole Essanay programme, English cinema managers had tried to impose a boycott on every American picture. But the boycott had collapsed. The rage of a public denied its favourite film-star was too great.

The story in the United States was not so encouraging. In May, Chaplin plummeted to thirty-sixth in the 'Popular Player Contest'. People began to predict the passing of the Chaplin vogue. The Mutual contract gnawed away at his screen image and made it appear faintly anomalous. It was hard to reconcile the near-millionaire with that underprivileged figure. The critics, as always, were in a quandary. In their attitude towards Chaplin's work, they had shown themselves equivocal; in their reaction to his new contract, they were painfully undecided. On the one hand, the promise of the 'Land of Opportunity' appeared to have been magnificently vindicated; on the other, the difficult question of excess cried out to be answered. Chaplin's money became an obsession, and at least one magazine in every month up to the end of the year contained an article, a letter, a reference or a cartoon about it. 'C. Chaplin, Millionaire-Elect', boomed one title in *Photoplay*.[17] 'If he continues in his frugal habits, Charles should be well on the way to millionairedom by 1917,' confided the writer, and then went on to compare Chaplin's salary with those of various government officials: the President and Vice-President, Chief Justice of the Supreme Court, Members of Congress, Senators and so on. He concluded that the Mutual contract was not only the biggest salary 'grabbed off' by any public person outside of royalty, but '93% of the payroll of the Senate, the most powerful legislative body in the world'. At this point his courage gave out. He had just used the term 'grabbed off', which was none too complimentary, he had just demonstrated that in the material scale of values, the President was of less worth than a film-star, he had by implication raised the question of economic justice. The waters were altogether too deep. With a flurry of foam he scrambled back to shore. The salary might sound wildly extravagant, but 'it falls into its proper relation in the scale of receipts and disbursements when the profits made out of Chaplin's pictures are considered'.

This playing about with figures was not as dangerous to Chaplin's reputation as was, perhaps, a racy, ironic and trenchant article that appeared in *Motion Picture Magazine*.[18] The strangest thing about it was its authorship. It had come from Robert Grau, a widely experienced and knowledgeable writer on the entertainment scene who was also an ardent fan of Chaplin's. He had once called him 'the most extraordinary figure the Motion Picture has ever revealed – not a mere fad, not a specialist, but a great artist'. Whether Grau intended his piece to do any harm will never be known, but phrases like 'ever since Chaplin arrived in New York in a deliberate plan to bankrupt the nation . . .' could not have gained the comedian any friends. Grau's theme was a neat twist on the idea that Chaplin's job was to make people laugh, only this time the joke was somewhat different. The whole film world was laughing uproariously at the 'truly funny spectacle of a screen star, two years ago hardly known by name, inducing a half-dozen sane film barons to pay him more money per week (and every week of the fifty-two in the year) than was ever meted out to Edwin Booth, Patti, Caruso and Paderewski in a job lot . . .'. Obviously, the longer Chaplin could make people laugh, the better he was performing his job as a comedian. As the loudest laughter was provoked through incredulity at the extraordinary salary he was demanding, the higher the salary the greater the laughter. Grau foretold a time when Chaplin would no longer create laughter on film, but would do so by keeping 'the people laughing at his contracts'. It was a clever and mischievous piece of writing. It ignored the fact that Sidney was the brain behind the business deal, and it suggested that the Chaplin brothers had performed an enormous hoax on the film producers like a couple of wily, unscrupulous insurance salesmen.

The next month Chaplin dropped still further in the 'Popular Player Contest' to forty-first. Essanay issued a news-letter which announced their victory in the courts against charges Chaplin had brought concerning their re-editing of *Carmen*. In turn, they were about to sue him for breach of contract to the tune of $500,000. His first two films for Mutual had been released to the type of mixed reviews which by then he must have become inured to. Louis Reeves Harrison, for the *Moving Picture World*, advocated once more the change critics had implored Chaplin to consider when he was with Essanay. 'Chaplin is an artist of larger capacity, of greater versatility than is apparent to those who know him best,' he declared.[19] 'He needs bigger opportunity, but his personality is so convincing that *The Floorwalker* will win and keep many an audience laughing after it is well under way.' But the *New York Dramatic Mirror* compared it favourably with the best of Chaplin's work. The public also took to it. A mood partly of cynicism, partly of dismay, had gripped the United States. There was talk of the enormous profits American manufacturers were making out of the war.

> The same old suffragettes hold forth,
> The same old war-talk bores,
> The same old stocks go up and down
> The same old weather pours,

wrote a contributor to *Motion Micture Magazine*, arguing that mirth such as Chaplin generated was at a premium at times like these.

Others were of the same opinion. From the war front he had received a steadily increasing stream of grateful letters and was on the way to becoming a folk-hero among the troops. At any lull in the fighting, long lines of them could be seen winding their way round the hastily erected cinema tents. 'It is impossible to make you realize how they were appreciated,' wrote a Major Murphy about the films his men had seen, 'and I truly wish you could have heard the shout that went up when Charlie appeared on the screen.'[20] Other letters from the wounded in hospitals, from battalions sailing to the war, flooded

'From the war front, Chaplin received a steadily increasing stream of grateful letters.' This card is dated 17 July 1916, and comes from Field Post Office No. 8. The sender, 'Curly', has drawn Chaplin on the front

into the studios. This might have seemed ample evidence of Chaplin's usefulness in doing what he was doing, but not to a growing crowd of vociferous attackers. The British Embassy in America, according to R. J. Minney,[21] had already told Chaplin that his services were of much more value to his country as a morale-booster for the troops than as a diminutive infantryman. But the vultures were not to be denied their feast. Their campaign grew and sly questions were asked in several editorials. However, it was to be some months before the campaign reached its climax.

The pressure on Chaplin mounted, not only from the war fever but from the swell of envy and hostility his last contract had provoked. 'I don't believe one word of all that stuff you say you heard about Chaplin,' wrote the 'Answer Man' in *Motion Picture Magazine*[22] in reply to a reader's letter. 'As soon as a person becomes famous, then the news-carriers get busy.' But the same edition carried a particularly pointed cartoon of Chaplin greedily eyeing the US Mint.

Reviews fortunately reflected nothing of the personal attacks upon him. In fact the most influential of the film magazines, *Photoplay*, made a point of calling him a genius, and even *Variety*, which had been almost consistently hostile, classed him as 'the world's champion high-priced film comic'.[23] There were, of course, the usual number of dissidents, the *Moving Picture World* returning to a theme which by that time could with some justification have been termed ancient. 'While this Chaplin effort will doubtless evoke much laughter from a

The Chaplin image was also used for propaganda purposes. These five cards come from the 'At the Front' series published by Geo. Pulman and Sons Ltd, London

certain class of audience,' it observed haughtily, 'it is not one to be strongly recommended. There is throughout a distinct vein of vulgarity which is unnecessary, even in slapstick comedy.'[24] On the whole, however, reviewers and public appear to have settled down to accepting Chaplin as the most formidable talent among screen comedians. In a strange way, the source of so much of his trouble – his huge salary – also acted as a kind of battle-honour, giving him a certain status even among his opponents. Friends, too, were springing up from the embattled ranks of the intellectuals and left-wing thinkers. He became a symbol of the innate good judgement of the masses. To 'anyone who loves an art and practises it', he was, as one journalist wrote, 'an example of how the best can be the most successful, and of how a real talent can triumph over the most appalling limitations put upon its expression, and of how the popular eye can recognize such a talent without the aid of the pundits of culture and even in spite of their anathemas'.[25]

Chaplin needed all such support during the coming months, for at the beginning of April 1917 the United States went to war and the campaign which had been smouldering against him suddenly erupted. Letters containing specific and detailed threats against him arrived at the studios, white feathers were sent through the post, and a storm of abuse was deliberately whipped up by sections of the press. His personal secretary tried to stop the letters from reaching him, but some of them got through and caused him deep and lasting distress. Quietly he went along to the recruiting office and was told he did not come up to the required physical standards of the US Army. His brother set about gathering a list of famous and influential signatures supporting Chaplin's position as a non-combatant, and managed to acquire more than a hundred. At last Chaplin was ready to make a statement. He repeated the argument that he was of more use at home than at the front, he declared himself a patriot (a description he was to renounce later) and a fighter for democracy. He had never courted publicity for his war efforts, and could have easily marched at the head of a column of reporters, critics and columnists to the nearest recruiting office, knowing full well the value of such a stunt. In fact he had gone along without anyone being told and had been declared underweight by the army doctors.

It was a long statement, much of it rhetorical. It was also a clever one. Without being in the least cynical about Chaplin's motives, one does feel that the story of his publicised visit to the recruiting office gained him more sympathy than if it had been accompanied with all the ballyhoo of the press. The result was that the campaign abated though it reappeared in a different guise years later at his political witch-hunt.

Thousands of letters supporting him flowed into his office and a nation-wide press took up his defence.

It was about this time that *The Immigrant* was released, and perhaps its slight disparagement of the way America received its new settlers was in part due to the bitterness engendered by what Chaplin had recently gone through. The film was a great and encouraging success, proof that his draw in the cinema had not weakened and that he was finding a fresh, radically minded audience. Julian Johnson in *Photoplay* considered it 'as much a jewel as a story by O. Henry . . .'.[26]

Chaplin followed it up in October with the last of his films for Mutual, *The Adventurer*. The title was unintentionally prophetic, for in a sense he was about to embark on the most difficult adventure of his life. He had entered into a contract with First National for a sum of $1,000,000 plus a $15,000 bonus on signing. He was to make eight pictures in eighteen months. He was to be his own producer with almost total control over his work. The screen character he had developed over the past three years had at last been granted its freedom of expression, but at the same time it had become the prisoner of big business. An era had passed in the life of the 'Little Fellow', and he was never to be quite the same again.

## 8. References

1. Lecture to Nottingham Playgoers' Club, 1925.
2. *Exhibitor's Mail*, February 1914.
3. *Moving Picture World*, June 1914.
4. Review of *The Property Man* in *Moving Picture World*, August 1914.
5. *Photoplay*, April 1915.
6. *Variety*, June 1915.
7. ibid.
8. *Little Review*, May 1915.
9. *Photoplay*, October 1915.
10. *Photoplay*, November 1915.
11. *Motion Picture Magazine*, September 1915.
12. *Photoplay*, January 1916.
13. *Photoplay*, March 1915.
14. *Motion Picture Magazine*, June 1915.
15. *Harper's Weekly*, 6 May 1916.
16. *Photoplay*, April 1916.
17. *Photoplay*, May 1916.
18. *Motion Picture Magazine*, May 1916.
17. *Photoplay*, May 1916.
18. *Motion Picture Magazine*, May 1916.
19. *Moving Picture World*, June 1916.
20. Langford Reed, *The Chronicles of Charlie Chaplin*, London: Cassell, 1917.
21. R. J. Minney, *Chaplin, the Immortal Tramp*, London: Newnes, 1954.
22. *Motion Picture Magazine*, August 1916.
23. *Variety*, November 1916.
24. Review of *Behind the Screen* in *Moving Picture World*, quoted by Mark Ricci in Gerald D. Macdonald, Michael Conway and Mark Ricci (eds.), *The Films of Charlie Chaplin*, New York: Bonanza Books, 1971.
25. Harvey O'Higgins in *New Republic*, 3 February 1917.
26. *Photoplay*, September 1917.

# Nine

'Masterpieces are not single and solitary births, they are the outcome of many years of thinking in common, of thinking by the body of the people, so that the experience of the mass is behind the single voice' – Virginia Woolf

Perhaps the most difficult problem facing anyone attempting to analyse Chaplin's screen persona is to detach the reality from the myth. The problem becomes even more complicated when the period under consideration involves only the years from Sennett to the end of the Mutual contract. Most of the ideas and theories attached to him were first thought of much later when he had already moved away from the broader comedy of those early days. Admiring critics who wrote about him in the 1920s or 1930s were themselves part-originators of the myth or subscribers to it – an indication, one suspects, of their own needs rather than the claims of the subject. It was very tempting at that time to interpret the Chaplin figure as a symbol of the human condition: his loneliness, his pathos, his resilience were those of modern man stripped of his old beliefs but quixotic and indomitable to the last. Though not a bad thing in itself, this type of attitude does tend to lose sight of the subject in a maze of abstractions.

The most common shibboleth among these critics was the label 'The Tramp'. Of all the terms by which Chaplin is described, this is, perhaps, the most misleading. The vagrants who roamed the London streets and slept along the Embankment at the turn of the century, and even well beyond it, would have found nothing in common with the portrait Chaplin projected on the screen. One genuine photograph of the real thing is enough. Cowed and beaten, the man stares out at us with a look of such utter resignation that the shock of his presence, even over a span of some eighty years, is as actual as if he were standing in the room facing us. The position of his hands with the palms wide open in a gesture of supplication means 'fie', the sign for final hopelessness. Chaplin never approaches such degradation. His character is aggressive, resourceful, jaunty. He is always clean-shaven and washed. There is no suggestion of dirty fingernails, grubby underwear, rotting

The vagrants who roamed the London streets at the turn of the century would not have recognized themselves in Chaplin's tramp.

Reality was too harsh for audiences who wanted to be entertained. This photograph shows a real tramp: resigned and utterly destitute

teeth, bad breath or rheumy eyes; his clothes never hang in tatters, his boots never gape open. Although he is a wanderer in *The Vagabond* and *The Tramp*, and perhaps in *The Champion*, nevertheless the fundamental rootlessness of the vagrant is as foreign to Chaplin's conception of the 'Little Fellow' as building a house is to a Bedouin. In the vast majority of all the films made between 1914 and 1917, the 'Little Fellow' is firmly established in either a job, a house, a hotel (*not* a doss-house) or a family. Certainly his background is never very

'There is no suggestion of dirty fingernails, grubby underwear or rotting teeth, bad breath or rheumy eyes in Chaplin's tramp. His clothes never hang in tatters, his boots never gape open.' In this shot from *The Tramp* (Essanay, 1915), both Chaplin and Bud Jamison are supposed to be tramps; Jamison is certainly more convincing

detailed nor very important to the film other than to provide jokes based on situation rather than character, but its vagueness is something shared by all the comics with whom he played. There is not a more fanciful creation than Eric Campbell, for example, who belongs to Gilbert and Sullivan opera and to nothing that exists in this world. Society, in fact, is needed by the 'Little Fellow', for it is essential to his functioning. Without it there would be no arena in which to perform, no props to play with, no obstacles to circumvent, no competition to stimulate him. Unlike a real tramp, who actively shuns society, the 'Little Fellow' actively pursues it and is even prepared to work for it.

Purely on the practical side, he could never have copied an actual tramp; too many of his films relied for their effect on his being allowed to mix with people for whom any social intercourse with a vagrant

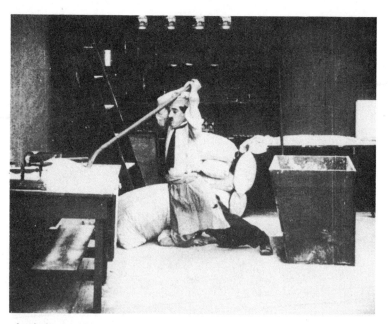

Chaplin's comedies are normally set in a familiar environment so that audiences can recognize the actions he is parodying or miming. Here we see him kneading the dough in *Dough and Dynamite* (Keystone, 1914) in a setting calculated to provide maximum comic potential

would have been unthinkable. Other men's wives had to ogle him, pretty maids to sympathize with him, businessmen to offer him a drink, butlers to serve him, wealthy girls to elope with him. Even the chance females he came across in the park, though not always respectable, were never slatternly and would have found the advances of a down-at-heel tramp disgusting. In fact Chaplin himself was sensitive of the need to keep accurately within class boundaries. When, in *The Vagabond*, he plays the part of an impoverished troubador, he makes certain that he creates the right social conditions for a credible romance by casting Edna Purviance as a gipsy. Clothes, another good indication of class, are always given special attention by him. *Those Love Pangs* shows Chester Conklin and himself as boarders at the same guest-house and as rivals for the same girls. There is nothing in the state of their dress to distinguish one from the other: baggy trousers, ill-fitting and creased jackets, large boots are common to both. In *Twenty Minutes of Love*, while flirting with a girl, he makes a furrow in the crown of his bowler to change it into a homburg, thereby giving him more status in her eyes and making it appear credible that the watch and chain he has stolen could really be his. Higher up the social scale he appears equally

In *Twenty Minutes of Love* (Keystone, 1914), 'while flirting with a girl, he makes a furrow in the crown of his bowler . . .'. Minta Durfee is the girl for whom Chaplin thinks it necessary to change his social standing

suitably dressed. When he is taken home by Edna Purviance and her mother after a chance meeting in the park, Chaplin's garb is not so incongruously out of place as to make nonsense of the occurrence. The more one explores the character of the 'Little Fellow', the more one realizes the importance that class played in its evolution.

Chaplin's costume is never incongruous enough to make complete nonsense of a particular situation. In this scene from *Caught in a Cabaret* (Keystone, 1914), he looks smart enough to be mistaken for the 'Premier of Greenland' by Mabel Normand, although he is only a waiter taking his dog for a walk

With this in mind, and having divested ourselves of any lingering thoughts about tramps and vagabonds, we can take a fresh look at what the character of the 'Little Fellow' actually meant for Chaplin. He has said on several occasions that they could have been two complete strangers who happened to lodge in the same apartment. But one should, perhaps, be wary of artists who claim diplomatic immunity from their own creation. The inspiration has to come from somewhere, and if the final result may show nothing or very little of the conscious day-to-day man, then there is every reason to suppose that the material has been supplied directly from the unconscious. The connection between the 'Little Fellow' and Chaplin is far too strong to be ignored.

The first point to be stressed, although an obvious one, is that his clothes were English. They may not have been made in England, or even bought there, but the way they were put together is as inescapably English as an empty Sunday afternoon. The expression is chosen advisedly, for the particular emptiness that comes to mind was at its drabbest in the suburbs of London at the turn of the century, and it was there that the 'Little Fellow' could be found. An array of them stood behind the counters of corn merchants and grocery shops and dairies. Others travelled up to Blackfriars or London Bridge every day and spent their working hours on a high stool in a back office checking columns of figures or sending out catalogues for mail-order firms. Wherever they went they carried the mark of their class, the lines of pallid street-lamps, the sullen rows of villas, the never-ending rattle of the railway line. Their origins were uncertain. Their fathers might have been comfortably off working men who employed a small staff of chimney sweeps or journeymen potters. They certainly would have had less education than their sons, who had learned to add and subtract, to write in a neat copperplate and to name some of the principal cities of the world. Their school had fitted them to be clerks and shop assistants. They served the middle classes, learned some of their ways, aped their conduct and dwelt in that pale, indeterminate region between the skilled artisan and the prosperous businessman known as the lower middle class.

No matter how Chaplin chose to present his 'Little Fellow', whether he gave him a fancy waistcoat or a tie, or whether he put him in torn trousers and shabby boots, the lower middle class was always his point of departure. It is strange indeed that this assortment of clothes, never assembled with any thought for personal expression, should have released so much of the inner life of the man wearing them. The process was gradual, as if Chaplin began tentatively with his new public and only gained confidence to show them more and more of himself as their affection for him grew. Perhaps he began to experience the heady exhilaration of discovering that some of the things he had been ashamed of, that he had suppressed or not even allowed to float to the surface, were admired, thought amusing, even loved. Having suffered from the stigma of his class – its lack of the social graces, its inadequate education, its pinched life-style, its slavish imitation of its betters – Chaplin suddenly found them in his late twenties transformed into some of his greatest assets. His weakness had become his strength.

To give one example. In *The Count*, while trying to pass himself off as an aristocrat, Chaplin is confronted with a large slice of melon which he obviously has to eat without giving himself away. At a loss what to do, he turns the situation into a joke – 'washing his ears in water-melon juice at the table', as the *Chicago Tribune* put it. If we, the

When Chaplin is confronted with such social predicaments as how to eat a water-melon, 'he turns the situation into a joke!' Here are three shots from this hilarious scene in *The Count* (Mutual, 1916). The other diners are Eric Campbell and Edna Purviance

audience, share in his plight, we laugh with relief that he has managed to avoid being humiliated; if, however, we are confident of our ability to cope with the problem, we laugh with satisfaction at the antics of someone who has made us feel superior. But either way he has amused us. How he has done so is by employing the same kind of technique a child might use to soften or deflect the disapproval of a parent who has demanded a certain standard which the child cannot meet. It performs a trick – be it a winsome smile or a roll on its belly – which never fails to disarm its parent. By substituting 'middle class' for 'parent', and 'Chaplin' for 'child', it is possible to see how the motive power for a typical piece of Chaplin business may originate in his own feelings of social inadequacy. Some of his best work is almost a straightforward reproduction of the type of conduct instilled into members of his class. For instance, one of his most characteristic and beguiling images was that of a man down on his luck being fastidiously correct over eating his food, even if it is no more than a battered sausage boiled in an old soup can. We laugh at the incongruity of the action, but it is only a reflection of the excessive emphasis the lower middle class placed on table manners and its determination to ape its superiors, no matter what the circumstances.

In this scene from *The Tramp* (Essanay, 1915), Chaplin fastidiously cleans his fingernails before embarking on a meal which renders such delicacy absurdly misplaced

Chaplin parodies etiquette by exaggerating it. In this scene from *The Immigrant* (Mutual, 1917), he tries to eat a plateful of peas one by one; but, exasperated by the futility of it all, ends by scooping them up in large piles with his fork.
The pained onlooker is Albert Austin

Once again, Chaplin finds humour in social convention. A washtub is turned into a table and Edna Purviance's smock serves as a tablecloth. Charlie then delicately forms the sleeves into napkins (*The Vagabond*, Mutual, 1916)

He would never have been able fully to develop this kind of humour, which is basically a conflict between reality and fantasy, had it not been for the conflict within himself.

This also gave rise to other aspects of the 'Little Fellow' which were not as immediately appealing, and in this connection the part played by his costume is crucial. There was obviously nothing new in wearing ill-fitting or extravagent articles of clothing, for we have already seen how the Commedia dell'Arte applied the idea; but whereas they had arrived at it after a process of experiment, Chaplin's costume began a process of experiment. By distorting the fashion of the lower-middle-class uniform, he had inadvertently provided an outlet for the frustrations and tensions that went with it. A physical change produced an imaginative change. It was as if a radio enthusiast, while tampering with the knobs and switches on his receiver, had suddenly tuned in to a powerful, alien sound-wave in the atmosphere.

Once discovered it proved irresistible. Emotions which would have appeared sinister or unpleasant in a character dressed normally were now not only liberated through the absurdity of Chaplin's garb, but were actually made acceptable by it. Thus the 'Little Fellow' could be unprincipled, lecherous, vulgar and violent – all the reactions of some-

Chaplin always had an eye for the female form, animate or inanimate. The speculative ogle for the animate comes from *The Count* (Mutual, 1916), and the coy furtiveness for the inanimate from *His New Job* (Essanay, 1915). Underlying both types of joke was a suggestiveness which might have proved more offensive with a less incongruous garb or situation

one breaking loose from a rigid conservatism – and still make people laugh. Obviously he was influenced by what Sennett expected of him and by some of the robust traditions of the Commedia he had inherited. But Chaplin went further than Sennett, while the Commedia was an example not a principal cause. His costume was the catalyst for something already in existence. Years after he was to describe what had happened when it worked its magic on him for the first time:

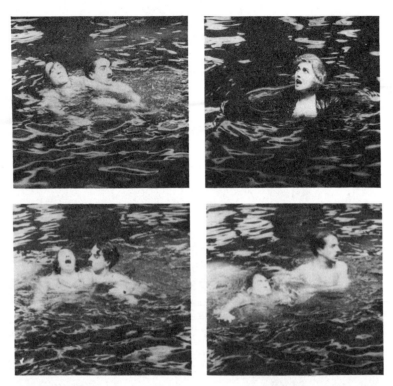

A further example of cruelty in
Chaplin's humour: in this scene from
*The Adventurer* (Mutual, 1917), he
leaves Marta Golden to drown as
soon as he sees that the attractive Edna
Purviance, her daughter, is also in
difficulties

The clothes seemed to imbue me with the spirit of the character.
He actually became a man with a soul – a point of view. I defended
to Mr Sennett the type of person he was. 'He wears an air of romantic
hunger, forever seeking romance, but his feet won't let him.'[1]

One wonders if he was also aware of how potently those large
ungainly boots expressed the handicaps of his early background, and if
he realized how much of the romantic hunger, the point of view and
the soul were his own.

Although Sennett was the first to hear of the 'Little Fellow's'
romantic leanings, it was not until a film like *The Bank*, which was
made with Essanay, that Chaplin was to give romance its head. Until
then his attitude towards women was of a piece with the other
characters who surrounded him. Girls were there simply to be pursued;
the hunt was not particularly marked by gallantry or respect beyond

the conventional demands of raising the hat and bowing with a broad smile. In *Laughing Gas*, for example, once the preliminary jousting is

'. . . the Little Fellow thinks nothing of swinging his leg over the lap of the recumbent girl patient'; *Laughing Gas* (Keystone, 1914)

over, the 'Little Fellow' thinks nothing of swinging his leg over the lap of the recumbent girl patient, as if irritated with the rules of the love game. However, underlying the coyness, the roguishness, the short flurries that the 'Little Fellow' brings to bear on his prey, there is evident a much more complicated impulse than the brazen directness of, say, Mack Swain, who is purely a womanizer, although an absurd one. An incident in *Shanghaied* serves to illustrate the point. Chaplin and Edna Purviance are carrying on a flirtation over a garden gate, when without warning he grabs her round the neck with his stick and

Chaplin often finds himself rescuing Edna from an unsuitable suitor. Here, in *The Adventurer* (Mutual, 1917), it is Eric Campbell, whose hideous beard makes him appear even more of a cad

pulls her head towards him. The kiss he delivers is passionless, almost chaste, but the next moment he wipes his lips clean. The whole sequence takes less than a minute, but it is sufficiently long to demonstrate just how far removed the 'Little Fellow's' motivation is from the outright lustfulness of slapstick. Judging by his brief encounter with Purviance, it was compounded of attraction and aggression, fear and distaste.

An earlier chapter went into Chaplin's tangled private problems with women as a result of his relationship with a mother whom he felt had abandoned him at the moment when he needed her most. All beautiful women thereafter were as much a threat as a temptation. Their affairs with him went through bewildering fluctuations of interest and indifference, suspicion and trust. It is clear that something like the same pattern of advance and retreat runs through the sequence in *Shanghaied* and leads one to conclude that the 'Little Fellow' inherited some of Chaplin's own problems.

Perhaps that was why he hastened towards romance. It was a way of eluding the warring instincts that rose up whenever his involvement

One of the most direct anti-romantic statements from the Keystone period is *The Face on the Bar-room Floor* (Keystone, 1914). A burlesque of a popular story, it tells of an artist whose loved one has run off with another man. Having regaled a bar full of customers with his tale, Chaplin then comes face to face with his former love (Cecile Arnold), who is now gross and saddled with several children. His reaction is a mixture of distaste and relief at having escaped a dreadful fate

with a woman was strongly earthbound. The 'Little Fellow' had found little encouragement for romance in his Sennett days. Not only was the whole tone of the films anti-romantic, but a volatile, shrewd comedienne like Mabel Normand could never have played Chaplin's idea of romance with absolute seriousness. With Edna Purviance the story was different. Here was a calm, malleable girl who could be turned into his heroine, his romantic ideal. It so happened that this idea

Mabel Normand's brand of comedy demanded a far less quixotic response from Chaplin than his later heroines were to receive. The 'joys' of family life are amply demonstrated in *His Trysting Place* (Keystone, 1914), a film which is once again decidedly unromantic

coincided with Chaplin's image of his mother, and so the result was predictable. Having to play opposite the Chaplin heroine, the 'Little Fellow' was once again saddled with his master's emotions. Only this time there was one essential difference: sexual love had given way to filial love. The 'Little Fellow' no longer desired his heroine, he worshipped her. And it is in films like *The Bank* and *The Vagabond*, in which romanticism is at its most intense, that this idolatry, as it were, reaches its peak.

As well as his first full expression of romanticism, *The Bank* has always been regarded as Chaplin's first real foray into pathos. The two events were almost bound to be simultaneous. Except for one film, *The Kid*, the periods when the 'Little Fellow' suffered grief or pain were always brought on by the loss, imminent or past, of a woman's love. It was the last step in an equation. Romance and a heroine cast in his mother's image could only lead in the end to a re-enactment of the deep sense of loss Chaplin had experienced as a child. Thus the pathos of the 'Little Fellow' when he wakes up in *The Bank* to find his adored one in the arms of the cashier, or when he sees her riding away with the artist in *The Vagabond*, or even in *The Tramp* (which is not as permeated with romanticism as the other two) as through a window he catches sight of Edna embracing her boy-friend –

all this delicate, gentle pathos has its roots in Chaplin's own childhood. It is also moments like these that people have in mind when they talk of the 'Little Fellow's' sensitivity or 'soul'. This is, perhaps, unavoidable. There is very little evidence, especially in the period under discussion, of the 'Little Fellow' extending the same kind of refinement towards men.

Chaplin's overtures to women were nearly always ambiguous: shy and tentative on the one hand, lewd and aggressive on the other. The two were never comfortably integrated. Shown here are three examples of his more restrained side. In the first, from *Work* (Essanay, 1915), he cleans his fingernails with a trowel while desperately trying to make conversation with Edna Purviance. The second, from *The Star Boarder* (Keystone, 1914), shows him gently disengaging Alice Davenport's dress from a bush. Finally, Chaplin coyly approaches a solitary girl on a bench in *Twenty Minutes of Love* (Keystone, 1914)

For his first admirers it was no real drawback. Pathos and sensitivity were not qualities they associated with him. In June 1915, *Motion Picture World* put out a series of cartoons of famous stars under the heading 'A Few Things That We Do Not Expect to See'. It included one of Chaplin in the role of Hamlet. *The Tramp* had been released a month before, but obviously its handling of pathos had gone unnoticed. Indeed, the pattern of Chaplin's success appears to show that the more serious the 'Little Fellow' became, the less he could rely on the support of his original audiences. A glance over the Chaplin cartoons from 1914 to 1917 reveals that the 'Little Fellow' appealed to his public neither as a romantic hero, nor even as a lonely waif, but simply as a likeable rogue. 'You're all right, Charlie! Hee! Hee!' chortles a cartoon representation of the globe, as with a wide grin it grasps Chaplin's hand. 'You're all right, you little rascal!'[2]

Roguery and rascality are as much a part of the 'Little Fellow's' make-up as his violence and vulgarity. There is hardly an occasion when he is not scoring off someone, kicking them or knocking them about (hardly ever with his fists, mostly with a weapon), by making them look foolish or clumsy, by outwitting them, by taking advantage of them. He is not averse to stealing the contents of a woman's handbag, as he does in *Mabel's Busy Day*, or picking someone's pocket, as in

Stealing from the unsuspecting is a common Chaplin pastime. Here he takes a handkerchief from a woman's handbag in *Mabel's Busy Day* (Keystone, 1914)

*In the Park.* He allows an old man to do all the work for him in *The Property Man*, repeatedly hits a patient over the head with a mallet in *Laughing Gas*, and throws acid in the face of his boss in *The Pawnshop*. In *Behind the Screen* he halts a pie-throwing fight by showing a white handkerchief, and when Eric Campbell moves out of cover imagining it to be a truce, hits him full in the face with another pie. It is all done with panache and agility and the victims help to soften the violence by reacting so unrealistically that no one could ever imagine them to be really hurt.

The response to these situations, however, was based on something more complex than an unsophisticated sense of humour. Chaplin himself said that had the 'Little Fellow' worked his tricks on a charwoman, for instance, then the joke would have misfired. She would have become an object of sympathy rather than derision. He might have profitably added that had the same charwoman taken herself too seriously and betrayed some of the foibles and pomposity of the petty bureaucracy, the 'Little Fellow's' guile would have been received with as much amusement as usual. The point is that a great deal of the 'Little Fellow's' appeal lay with his battle against authority – not necessarily vested authority, but anything that was inherently presumptuous, rooted in the belief that some people deserve more than others. For those who had fled Europe for America, authority in any shape was automatically suspect. The sweat-shops, carnivorous landlords, street gangs, organized crime and corrupt laywers that greeted them in their new country did nothing to dispel their fears. Over and above that it was an age of creeping disillusionment. The First World War was gradually putting paid to old assumptions about merit, respect for law, a national 'way of life' and the benefits of civilization. Even before the war the decay of society had been bemoaned by writers like Max Nordau who insisted in *Degeneration* (1893) that it was, 'Marching to its certain ruin because it is too worn out and flaccid to perform great tasks.' The result among ordinary people was a kind of cynical egalitarianism: everyone was the same underneath, and those who tried to stand out from the herd or to arrogate to themselves status or pride were guilty of one more of society's sins – hypocrisy.

The 'Little Fellow' was never a hypocrite, whereas a large number of those whom he used and made fools of were. The respectable husbands who fought for his attentions when he dressed up as a woman (*A Woman*) were every bit as lascivious as he, but not as honest about it. The father who welcomed him as a prospective son-

In the several films in which he posed as a woman, Chaplin succeeded in turning many a male head. Here he is in *The Masquerader* (Keystone, 1914), attracting the attention of Charlie Murray. In *A Woman* (Essanay, 1915), it is Charles Insley who looks at the female Chaplin lasciviously

in-law when in *The Jitney Elopement* he masqueraded as a count, was just as much a social climber as the 'Little Fellow', but would never have admitted it. And so, in his encounters with the rich and the privileged, he could be as devious and unprincipled as he wished, knowing full well that by their hypocrisy they had forfeited any sympathy whereas in comparison he appeared almost blameless.

*9. References*

1 *Woman's Home Companion*, November 1933.
2. *Motion Picture Magazine*, June 1915.

# Ten

'Objects have no discoverable connexion together; nor is it from any other principle but custom operating upon the imagination, that we can draw any inference from the appearance of one to the experience of another' – David Hume, *Treatise on Human Nature* (1739–40)

The quality that made Chaplin unique among silent screen comedians is as elusive as a scent that stirs a forgotten childhood memory. Part of the problem of trying to define it arises from the fact that so many influences are at work on the 'Little Fellow' that he seems less the creation of one man than of countless generations, the culmination of many comic traditions. Nevertheless, even though we may not be able to put a name to it, we do recognize that a consistent attitude towards the world of objects and humans lies behind the apparent contradictions in his behaviour. That attitude becomes clearer once we begin to summarize those aspects of the 'Little Fellow' which he shared in common with other comic figures of the time and which were also part of his professional experience. When he began filming he had already been a popular entertainer for something like fifteen years and one must assume that such a long period had left him a considerable legacy of ideas and technique.

Of paramount importance was the influence of Fred Karno. Relatively little remains of Karno's sketches beyond a few short scripts and the recorded memories of those who worked for him. A wealth of detail about the type of business his actors were instructed to perform has been lost. To gauge just how far Chaplin was indebted to him poses considerable problems. There were some who thought that he owed almost everything to Karno. Hal Roach, who knew at first-hand how both of them worked, commented:

> The eating of the shoes in *The Gold Rush*, that was an old vaude-ville thing that had already been done. The house on the cliff had already been done. As soon as Charlie had exhausted the great material he had gathered over the years working for Fred Karno, then his pictures and he started to go down.[1]*

*Roach failed to mention that the famous dance of the two bread rolls in *The Gold Rush* was probably copied from the famous music-hall comedian G. H. Chirgwin, who would impersonate a dancer by playing with two clay pipes on a tin tray.

Karno, as we have already noted, taught his players the trick of a sudden switch from comedy to pathos. He was an accomplished mime, he exploited oddities in dress and behaviour, his humour was often cruel and his tough training as an acrobat allowed him to devise and execute long sequences of complicated, adroit slapstick. All of this can be seen in Chaplin. The clever series of trips and falls and leapfrogs that he and Ben Turpin perform as they try to barge through the casting manager's door in *His New Job* were most probably a direct outcome of Karno's tuition. On the other hand, cruel humour, which Chaplin never quite shook off throughout his career, was not entirely a result of Karno's influence, for it was as much part of Chaplin's own personality as of his stage experience. The same holds true for pathos; when and how the 'Little Fellow' used it was very much the affair of his creator, despite the fact that Karno drilled it into all his players. However, the qualities of cruelty and pathos were not unique to Chaplin. Many of 'Fatty' Arbuckle's films suffer from moments of cruelty, and pathos was an essential part of John Bunny's screen personality. In the music hall, of course, pathos had long been considered a natural ingredient of any great comedian's act, and performers like Dan Leno and Albert Chevalier were masters at suspending an audience between sadness and mirth.

Exploiting oddities of dress and behaviour was purely traditional and in no way an original invention of either Karno or Chaplin. The 'Little Fellow's' big boots and queer walk might have been directly inspired by Fred Kitchen, but they were also part of the European comedy tradition that gave Pantaloon his long tapering slippers, and Pulcinella his odd hop and skip. More important for Chaplin was Kitchen's great skill as a mime. He undoubtedly acted as a model for the budding comedian, and gave him valuable guidance. Nevertheless he had fertile ground on which to sow. Chaplin's gifts had already been apparent when he played a 'dude' with a troupe of young clog-dancers called 'The Eight Lancashire Lads'. Later on he caused a mild sensation with his impersonation of 'Dr' Walford Bodie, the famous music-hall electrical healer and hypnotist. But one cannot claim that Chaplin as a mime was unique among screen comedians; the ground had been prepared beforehand, and Linder especially was his equal.

So far we have confined ourselves to discussing the more general ways by which the Karno years left their mark on Chaplin. As far as details are concerned, the task becomes much more difficult. If, as Hal Roach alleges, Chaplin roamed freely through the Karno storehouse for the raw material of his own productions, then one really ought to see its contents. Information, as has been noted, is scanty, but there are some interesting facts which, though small in themselves, assume some

I'M FAIRLY AMONGST THE GIRLS.

A postcard from the skating-craze era and a still from *The Rink* (Mutual, 1916) show the same brand of humour. With Chaplin are Eric Campbell and Albert Austin. Based on a sketch for Fred Karno partly written by Sydney Chaplin, *The Rink* gave Charlie an opportunity to exploit all the techniques he had learned in the music hall

significance when taken together. Chaplin toured for a time in a Karno sketch partly written by Sydney Chaplin and called *Skating*, the sport being a craze in England in 1909; this probably gave rise to *The Rink*.

A piece entitled 'Repairs', in which the two Chaplins appeared with a team of 'paper-hangers, painters and plumbers, all busy at the same time with buckets of paste and whitewash in the same room',[2] may well have been the stimulus for *Work*. *Jimmy the Fearless*, another

A traditional music-hall sketch featuring incompetent decorators was the basis for *Work* (Essanay, 1915).

Charlie's unfortunate boss is Charles Insley

Karno sketch, featured a romantic working-class lad who is rudely awakened from a dream of rescuing a damsel in distress; it is an idea which recurs in a slightly changed form in *The Bank* when Chaplin, as the caretaker who has just rescued a girl from a band of robbers, wakes up to find himself kissing a mop instead of her. A primitive Karno concoction named 'The Boxing Ball' featured an actor who was repeatedly hit in the face with a rebounding punch-ball; in *The*

This romantic shot from *The Bank* (Essanay, 1915) serves to highlight the contrast when Charlie wakes up and finds himself kissing, not Edna Purviance, but a mop

*Champion*, Chaplin keeps striking Leo White while sparring and playing with a swinging punch-ball. The centrepiece of *Wontdetainia*, a Karno diversion which ran at the Paragon, Mile End, in 1910, was a set which actually rolled like a huge ship on the high seas and provided a stream of stock music-hall jokes on seasickness; for *Shanghaied* and *The Immigrant*, Chaplin used a real ship but exploited the same type of humour. A lowly dental assistant who takes the place of his employer and performs extractions on his unwitting patients formed the central joke of Karno's 'The Dentist', and was the starting-point for Chaplin's *Laughing Gas*. Much used by Karno was a swing door which sprang back and hit anyone passing through, a prop which Chaplin first used in *His Favorite Pastime*. In 'Hilarity', Karno introduced a siphon which spurted a powerful jet of soda into the face of the luckless actor who picked it up; slightly adapted, it found its way into *His New Job*, *The Jitney Elopement*, *One A.M.*, *A Woman* and many other Chaplin films.

Albert Austin, the butler, looks on scandalized as Charlie squirts soda into a bottle of whisky in *The Adventurer* (Mutual, 1917), and thus adds one more to his list of social bloomers

There are other similarities. The 'Inebriated Swell' in *Mumming Birds* tries to light a cigarette from an electric bulb just outside his theatre box; as a drunken swell in *One A.M.* Chaplin attempts to light his cigarette from an electric lamp hanging from the ceiling. A sketch named *The G.P.O.*, starring Fred Kitchen as Perkins, contained an incident exactly reproduced by Chaplin several years later in a different setting. These are the stage directions for the Karno sketch just after a doctor has walked into the post office and bought a stamp:

> Turns from counter and sees Perkins, goes to him, pulls out watch, holds Perkins' wrist, taking pulse. Motions for him to put his tongue out. When Perkins does this, Doctor wets stamp on Perkins' tongue, sticks it on letter, looks him up and down, raises hat and walks out.[3]

Compare this with the following incident from *The Bank*: Chaplin has been sent to post a letter. He turns a corner and sees a client who has just been refused a loan leaning on a counter, looking ill. He stops and stares at him. He takes his pulse, looks at him again, turns the man's head with two fingers, forces him to put out his tongue, wets the stamps on it and sticks them on the envelope. With his tongue still hanging out, the man stares stupidly at Chaplin as he doffs his cap and leaves.

Parallels such as these must provoke the suspicion that Chaplin copied Karno much more than has ever been realized. For a last example, one may perhaps be forgiven for trespassing into a period beyond the province of this book. Karno was very fond of relating how, in his early days as an unsuccessful glazier, he would persuade a colleague to break a few windows and then miraculously arrive at the street door offering to replace them. *The Kid*, of course, uses the identical idea.

Music hall, as distinct from Karno, proved another great help for Chaplin's invention. The trend among great comedians like Robey, Chevalier and Leno was to develop a characteristic and simplified style which grew so familiar to people that a rapport between the artiste and his audience was created even before he strode on to the stage. Leno was particularly adept at establishing this kind of sympathy. His sudden and wild leaps on the stage, his exuberant entrance, his monkey-like features with their arched eyebrows and large, sad eyes, stamped him at once as the archetypal cockney urchin. He, too, was a wonderful mime, using hardly any props or scenery, but capable of peopling the stage with a crowd of imaginary and vivid characters. Like Chaplin, he was defiant, jaunty and sorrowful, and the screen comedian's instinctive search for a persona was directly inspired by Leno as well as by the music hall. In fact the *Bioscope* once called Chaplin 'the Dan Leno of the screen'.

Perhaps nothing can better capture Leno's luminous talent than Max Beerbohm's description of him as the shoemaker. One must bear in mind that there is no one on stage except Leno.

Dan Leno as 'The Ratcatcher', a
vivid characterization selected from
among an extensive gallery

The desperate hopefulness with which he adapted his manner to his different customers! One of his customers was a lady with her little boy. Dan Leno, skipping forward to meet her, with a peculiar skip invented specially for his performance, suddenly paused, stepped back several feet in one stride, eyeing the lady in wild amazement. He had never seen such a lovely child. *How* old, did the mother say? Three? He would have guessed seven at least – 'except when I look at you, ma'am, and then I should say he was one at most'. Here Dan Leno bent down, one hand on each knee, and began to talk some unimaginable kind of baby-language ... A little pair of red boots with white buttons? Dan Leno skipped towards an imaginary shelf; but in the middle of his skip, he paused, looked back, as though drawn by some irresistible attraction and began to talk to the child. As it turned out, he had no boots of the kind required. He plied the mother with other samples, suggested this and that, faintlier and faintlier, as he bowed her out. For a few moments he stood gazing after her, with blank disappointment, still bowing automatically. Then suddenly he burst out into a volley of deadly criticisms on the child's personal appearance, ceasing as suddenly at the entrance of another customer . . .[4]

The charm, the cunning, the delicacy and the insults could have been the 'Little Fellow's'. Even the sudden switch from flattery to hostility is echoed in the sequence in *The Fatal Mallet* when, having grown tired of Mabel Normand's disdainful reception of his advances, Chaplin suddenly delivers a swift kick to her behind.

'. . . Chaplin suddenly delivers a swift kick to her behind' (*The Fatal Mallet*, Keystone, 1914)

As music-hall comedians cultivated a familiar and consistent character, so they made use of catch phrases like Fred Kitchen's 'Meredith, we're in!' and repeated business and gags – a habit which seems to have made an audience feel secure and full of eager antici-pation. Chaplin slipped naturally into the format. His hat and his cane became his catch phrases. An audience expected him to doff his bowler as he bumped into someone's backside or as he fell over a step. They

A recumbent Chester Conklin is paid the dubious honour of having his bottom saluted by Chaplin in *Those Love Pangs* (Keystone, 1914)

were familiar with the way his cane would suddenly snake out and grasp an innocent bystander round the neck, or knock off an opponent's hat before tripping him up. They were overjoyed when the 'Little

The ever-watchful cane has flashed out and grasped Chester Conklin round the neck in *Mabel at the Wheel* (Keystone, 1914). Chaplin is wearing the costume of a 'swell', the part he played in *Mumming Birds*

Albert Austin as the shop assistant tries to cope with the confusion caused by the obstreperous Charlie, who unconcernedly hangs his cane on the store inspector's cigar in *The Floorwalker* (Mutual, 1916)

Fellow' hung it on a detective's pipe, as in *The Floorwalker*, or hooked it on a butler's waistcoat, as in *The Jitney Elopement*. They did not mind that gags were repeated, but on the contrary, welcomed them like old friends. And there were numerous occasions for them to do so. Chaplin unerringly swings his fob watch into the pocket of his waistcoat with barely a glance in *Those Love Pangs* and *Twenty Minutes of Love*. He picks his teeth with a pistol in *A Film Johnnie* and in *The New Janitor*. He keeps a crook covered with a gun from between his legs as he bends down to pick up something in *The Immigrant* and *The New Janitor*. He oils his muscles in *His Musical Career* and *Behind the Screen*. There are

Chaplin's cane evolved into a symbol which expressed a wide range of attitudes and qualities. In *The Jitney Elopement* (Essanay, 1915) it is hooked on to the waistcoat of the footman (Lloyd Bacon) with an effrontery that amazes Edna Purviance and her father (Fred Goodwins). Faced with his social betters (Alice Davenport, Hank Mann, Mabel Normand), Charlie nonchalantly hooks his cane in his pocket so as to shake hands in *Caught in a Cabaret* (Keystone, 1914). Finally, with appetite aroused, Charlie's cane sneaks out and grasps Phyllis Allen's thighs in *His Trysting Place* (Keystone, 1914)

The famous scene from *The New Janitor* (Keystone, 1914) when Charlie covers a crook with a gun from between his legs

The trapdoor in *Dough and Dynamite* (Keystone, 1914) and the sliding doors which grip Eric Campbell's head in *The Adventurer* (Mutual, 1917) are variations on an idea which occurs in several of Chaplin's films

sequences of people's heads caught between either trap-doors or sliding doors in *Dough and Dynamite*, *Behind the Screen* and *The Adventurer*. Heavy sacks of flour are dropped on bosses and workmates in *Dough and Dynamite* and *The Tramp*. Washing up the dishes in *Shanghaied* and *Dough and Dynamite*, he just drops them where he stands, completely unperturbed.

Gags would also reappear in a slightly changed form. In *Gentlemen of Nerve* he is sitting next to a girl with a bottle of lemonade; every time she turns to watch the motor race he takes a sip through her straw. In *Behind the Screen*, Albert Austin is gnawing at a bone which is

'. . . Albert Austin is gnawing at a bone which is dangling under Chaplin's nose.' The boss of the stage hands, Eric Campbell, glowers at his new worker while guzzling an enormous pile of pies in *Behind the Screen* (Mutual, 1916)

dangling under Chaplin's nose; every time Austin turns away, Chaplin claps two slices of bread over the end and takes a bite at it. He and Mack Swain are sitting in a donkey-cart loaded with a piano in *His Musical Career*: when the cart comes to a halt, the weight of the load forces down one end and hauls the donkey into the air between the shafts. The same gag crops up in *Work* with a clever variation. Chaplin is dragging a cart carrying his boss and a heap of decorating equipment. They come to a steep hill. Chaplin loses his footing and the cart begins to roll backwards. In an extreme long-shot, we see it accelerating downhill with Chaplin thrown up in the air kicking his legs like a trapped insect.

'. . . hauls a donkey into the air between the shafts'; *His Musical Career* (Keystone, 1914)

The horizon shot in *Work* (Essanay, 1915) shows Chaplin at his imaginative best. The striking image of Chaplin as a slave between the shafts of a cart driven by Charles Insley is a disturbing and bizarre opening to a film which is otherwise fairly predictable slapstick.

Another trick was to repeat the same gag several times within one film. It was a favourite device of Chaplin's which also had its roots in music hall. Fred Kitchen playing a bailiff constantly thrown out of the house he is trying to enter was an extremely popular sketch at the turn of the century. It was also a good example of the way in which a music-hall comedian could work up his audience's anticipation. Chaplin made use of the same technique. It is inevitable that every time he walks through the revolving doors in *The Cure* he will be whirled round and round like a Catherine-wheel; it is also certain that the camera tripod in *Behind the Screen* will give him trouble as often as he tries to pass round it. He sits on a hatpin several times in *A Woman*, and *Work* contains a delightful sequence in which the woman of the house, indicating with flamboyant gestures where the decorations need to be done, continually knocks Chaplin's bowler askew.

Music hall did not only repeat gags. It returned to the same jocular subjects again and again. Max Beerbohm gave a list of them: mothers-in-law; hen-pecked husbands; twins; old maids; Jews, Frenchmen, Germans, Italians, Negroes (not Russians, or other foreigners of any denomination); fatness, thinness, long hair (worn by a man), baldness; seasickness; stuttering; bad cheese; 'shooting the moon' (slang expression for leaving a lodging house without paying the bill).[5] Some of these subjects Chaplin brought into his films. Hen-pecked husbands with hefty, jealous wives appear in *Mabel's Strange Predicament*, *The Rounders*, *His Trysting Place* and *Getting Acquainted*. An early film, *A Busy Day*, features Chaplin himself playing a rather coarse, aggressive wife and Mack Swain the hen-pecked but flirtatious husband.

The closest Chaplin came to making use of the ancient comic contrivance of twins was in *The Floorwalker*. The actual floorwalker, who is made up to look uncannily like Chaplin, steals money from the store's safe, and on his way out comes face to face with his double. To divert his pursuers, he persuades Chaplin to take the bag of loot, and in the ensuing confusion Chaplin is mistaken for the thief.

When it came to foreigners, Chaplin was most fascinated by the French. Whenever he could, even on the slightest pretext, he introduced a Frenchman into his films. Leo White played nearly all of them. He was identified by his curling moustache and short beard, a topper, an air of outraged elegance and a strong supply of amorousness. Negroes appeared less frequently. Having followed a pretty girl home in *His Favourite Pastime*, Chaplin is well on the way to conquering her with his charm when he discovers to his horror that he has been making love to her Negro maid. *The Rounders* provides us with a brief glimpse of a Negro doorman at a night-club. Chaplin and Arbuckle quite capriciously knock off his hat and trip him up. A caricature of a

Chaplin and his twin, Lloyd Bacon, confront each other in *The Floorwalker* (Mutual, 1916) in a scene reminiscent of the kind of situation shown on the cover of a music-hall song sheet

Jewish doss-house owner makes an appearance in *Police*, and a German band plays outside a pub in *The Vagabond*.

Chaplin's fat men were either Henry Bergmann or Mack Swain, who was billed as 'Mr Stout' in *The Rink*. Arbuckle filled the role on several occasions. He is the furious husband of the girl Chaplin pursues in *His Favorite Pastime* and Chaplin's drinking partner in *The Rounders*. Thinness was personified by Albert Austin, a lanky dolorous-looking recruit from Karno's company. He is the bewildered man who stands helplessly looking on as Chaplin dissects his clock in *The Pawnshop*.

The Jewish doss-house owner in *Police* (Essanay, 1916) is played by Leo White, usually far more elegant as the lascivious dandy which was Chaplin's conception of a Frenchman

Eric Campbell as Mr Stout in *The Rink* (Mutual, 1916)

The celebrated sequence from *The Pawnshop* (Mutual, 1916) when Chaplin dissects a clock

Notwithstanding the number of jokes that the music hall could squeeze from the sight of long hair and baldness, Chaplin does not give them much prominence. An old-time actor from melodrama wearing hair down to his collar strides into the agent's office in *His New Job*, but, generally speaking, Chaplin transmuted long hair into ridiculously long false beards which hung from the most unlikely faces. The cameraman in *Behind the Screen*, though obviously a young man, sports one. Albert Austin as a waiter in *The Rink* looks distinctly grotesque in a Father Time beard, and, for some unaccountable reason, two gentlemen waiting for a massage in *The Cure* sit with straggling beards almost down to their waists. In contrast, baldness took a positive role, for it was used as a prop. In *The Rounders* Chaplin strikes a match against the bald head of a restaurant diner, and in *A Night in the Show* he repeats the same gag with a bald euphonium player seated in the orchestra pit. The only real contrast made between long hair and baldness occurs in *A Woman* in which the tonsured Charles Insley and the mop-haired Billy Armstrong fight for the attentions of Chaplin, dressed as an alluring female.

Shanghaied* and *The Immigrant* lent themselves naturally to jokes about seasickness; most of the first and nearly half of the second film takes place aboard a ship. In *Shanghaied*, Chaplin has to share a meal in a small cabin with the foul-mannered members of the crew. He is already queasy when he sits down at the heaving table, but when the mate drenches his meal with lamp-oil, Chaplin finds it too much and

As the tipsy attendant in *The Cure* (Mutual, 1917), James T. Kelley sports a beard which not only fits badly but is also quite inappropriate to the role

In his very first film, Chaplin showed many of the characteristics which were to remain with him for most of his career. Using a part of another person's body as a prop was one favourite technique. In *Making a Living* (Keystone, 1914), he exploits the baldness of the newspaper proprietor; and in *Triple Trouble* (Essanay, released 1918), he strikes a match against the foot of a sleeping tramp bolts for the door. The sequence is noteworthy for the way Chaplin exploits the idea of the plates sliding from one end of the table to the other, the sudden placing of his hat over a fork which carries a piece of evil-smelling meat, and for the fastidiousness of his gestures and expressions as he tries to fight his growing revulsion.

Fastidiousness is not the hallmark of *The Immigrant*, although the first joke may lead one to believe so. It shows Chaplin leaning over the ship's rail as it sways against the horizon. But he straightens up, turns round, and we realize he has only been fishing. The remaining jokes on seasickness are far less subtle. Chaplin narrowly escapes the vomit of a burly Russian, only to run into a vomiting youth. Stray shreds of

Albert Austin as the bearded Russian
who causes Charlie so much trouble
in *The Immigrant* (Mutual, 1917)

his food are carried by the wind on to Chaplin's bowler. Once again Chaplin flees, but rushes straight into the path of the Russian who dutifully obliges with another deluge of food. Chaplin finds a sheltered spot and squats down. The Russian follows, sits down beside him and in attempting to hold down the contents of his stomach, infects Chaplin with the same nausea. The sequence is long and distasteful.

Finally, bad cheese. It appears in *His Favorite Pastime* and in *The Count*. To escape a jealous husband in the first film, Chaplin shins up a telegraph pole. The husband finds a huge axe and proceeds to chop the pole down. In a burst of inspiration, Chaplin lowers a rancid piece of Limburger on the end of a long piece of string, and the enemy is routed. (He was to use Limburger again in *Shoulder Arms*, when he thwarts an impending German attack by hurling a cheese out of his trench into the enemy lines.) For *The Count*, Chaplin makes use of an odorous Camembert left in the kitchen of a rich household. To make sure that we anticipate the action, the butler gives the cook instructions to destroy the disgusting thing. Chaplin arrives to flirt with the cook and to cadge a meal – a state of affairs which, as noted in an earlier chapter, usually existed in the music hall between the cook and the local constable. Inadvertently Chaplin's fingers brush against the cheese and a moment later travel up to his moustache. The smell

The cook (Eva Thatcher) looks on
indulgently as Charlie samples the
cheese in *The Count* (Mutual, 1916)

almost overwhelms him. The cook hears the butler approaching, and in a panic hides her lover and the evidence of his meal in a convenient laundry hamper. Unhappily for Chaplin she also includes the cheese. He opens the lid for air several times until, unable to bear the torture any longer, he throws out the cheese. Naturally it knocks the butler to the floor.

Chaplin could not but be influenced by these music-hall plots and traditions. The proscenium arch is never entirely absent from all his work, in his early films especially; but even a comparatively late film like *One A.M.* is a straightforward recording of a music-hall solo act.

The camera never moves, the film is shot from the viewpoint of someone sitting in the stalls, and the framing is pure stage framing. 'Every picture that he made always had one particular high light,' stated his cameraman, 'Rollie' Totheroh, 'a good built-up spot to rock the house with it.'[6] This was merely a reflection of the way a typical slapstick sketch was constructed. Brief and snappy as it was, it nevertheless always moved towards a resounding climax. In trying to transpose the same method to the screen, Chaplin was faced with a medium that devoured time. Twenty minutes or so of comedy could not be sustained on the basis of a gradual build up towards one climax. As he invariably visualized the climax or 'high-light' before anything else, he had to find ways of filling up the time on either side of it. Unable to change his thinking entirely, he settled for minor climaxes, the little episodes of business we all recall when we think of a Chaplin film, the 'inspired moments' as Thomas Burke chose to call them. Unfortunately, this was no way by which to build an organic unity, and most of his films are marred by bad construction. Critics were very quick to point out how much Chaplin needed a good script-writer.

Either from lack of confidence or from Sennett's insistence on pace, the early films tend to be too full of minor business. Gags are hurried and clumsily set up. One hardly has time to grasp them before they are over. It was only as he began to control his medium that Chaplin came to understand the advantage of pacing out his gags. They were still subsidiary climaxes, but by giving them more detail he avoided the desperate hurry of his early work, gave time for his audience to appreciate his inventiveness, and conserved his material before exhausting it too quickly. He could also elaborate on gags he had used before. In *Work* he staggers up the stairs of a house loaded with all the decorating equipment he has been dragging along for miles. In *His Musical Career* he is forced to carry an upright piano on his back. Both gags are incorporated in *Behind the Screen*, but with far greater artistry. Instead of decorating equipment, Chaplin slings eleven chairs over his arm and across his back, and looking like a porcupine walks into the next set. Nonchalantly he picks up an upright

'. . . he is forced to carry an upright piano on his back.' Mack Swain takes refreshment while Charlie does the work in *His Musical Career* (Keystone, 1914)

piano and continues on his way. *His New Job* contains a sequence in which Chaplin knocks over a plaster pillar on the film set, tries to steady it and finally ends up with it on top of him. The whole sequence takes forty-eight seconds. Once again, *Behind the Screen* contains the

Ben Turpin makes sure that Charlie receives the full weight of a set pillar in *His New Job* (Essanay, 1915), while director Henry Bergman and his leading lady (Charlotte Mineau) stand by, powerless to stop the havoc

same gag but at far greater length and with more variety. Chaplin is told to set up a historical scene. He tries to pick up a massive plaster pillar, finds it too heavy, and propels it towards the set. It hits the director over the head, totters and causes panic among the actors, falls into an adjoining kitchen set and crashes to the ground knocking out Chaplin on the way. The sequence is one minute forty seconds long; but it is by no means the climax. A pie-throwing fight which leads into a hilarious sequence centred on a lever-operated trapdoor forms the real 'built-up spot' of the film.

The setting of *Behind the Screen* gave Chaplin the chance to use a wide selection of props, and was probably deliberately chosen for that purpose. It was also another example of how far he was indebted to tradition. The Commedia dell'Arte, as we have seen, chose its locations with the same aim in mind. Chaplin was addicted to the practice. *The Pawnshop* provided him with an arsenal of potentially interesting objects; the seedy music hall in *The Property Man* was liberal with gifts like artiste's luggage and effects; the dentist's studio in *Laughing Gas* supplied him with one of the most ancient of comic props – the enormous pliers with which he terrifies his patient. Il Dottore was

'. . . the enormous pliers with which he terrifies his patient.' *Laughing Gas* (Keystone, 1914) gave Chaplin every opportunity to play in the broad tradition of the Commedia dell' Arte

brandishing them more than 200 years before Chaplin. Indeed, props and sets proved of enormous importance for Chaplin's creative dynamism and were very often the only way to set it working. He built a studio street styled to evoke the atmosphere of a South London slum long before he knew how he was going to use it. It stood idle for several weeks before triggering off the childhood associations which led to *Easy Street*.

One of Chaplin's most polished films, *Easy Street* (Mutual, 1917) might have been shot in a slum in London rather than a film set in Hollywood. Here the diminutive new cop takes stock of the local villain, Eric Campbell

But the Commedia's influence did not extend to props alone. Somatic or body gags were as much a part of Chaplin's armour as they were of the *lazzi*. He sits on a hot stove in *The Vagabond* and burns himself against a radiator as he bends down to tie his shoelace in *His New Job*. He impales his rear on a helmet spike in *Behind the Screen*,

The implicit comedy of the human bottom was, as we saw earlier (p. 117), a temptation Chaplin hardly ever resisted. Here in *Those Love*

*Pangs* (Keystone, 1914), he puts paid to Chester Conklin's progress with the landlady with a well-judged thrust of his fork

sticks a fork into Chester Conklin's rump in *Those Love Pangs* and thrusts a sword into Henry Bergman's capacious behind in *His New Job*. He rubs bottoms with a rich, affronted lady in the hotel foyer of *A Night Out*, moves aside and punctiliously replaces a protuding behind in *The Bank* (a gag already used in *The Face on the Bar-room Floor*) and indulges in a wild backside-kicking duel with Eric Campbell in *The Count* which ends with both of them meting out the same treatment to their dancing partners. Chester Conklin has his nose bitten in *Gentlemen of Nerve*, while Lloyd Bacon has his wrist bitten in *In the Park*.

*In the Park* (Essanay, 1915) was by no means the first time Charlie bit someone's wrist. He did the same thing to Henry Lehrman in *Making a Living* (Keystone, 1914), thirty-eight films previously

Chaplin strikes a match against Ben Turpin's neck in *His New Job*, leans on a butler's shoulder in *A Jitney Elopement* and tries to sit on Edna Purviance as she bends to put a key in the door of her hotel room in *A Night Out*. The kicks Chaplin delivers to stomachs, shins and faces are legion, and would have been utterly familiar to any Commedia player. Even swinging a leg across a girl's lap or vaulting into the arms of a man about to hit him were part of Harlequin's repertoire long before Chaplin brought them to the screen.

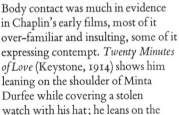

Body contact was much in evidence in Chaplin's early films, most of it over-familiar and insulting, some of it expressing contempt. *Twenty Minutes of Love* (Keystone, 1914) shows him leaning on the shoulder of Minta Durfee while covering a stolen watch with his hat; he leans on the shoulder of a lady spectator in *Mabel's Busy Day* (Keystone, 1914); rests against Mack Swain's bottom in *Mabel's Married Life* (Keystone, 1914); places one foot in Edna Purviance's lap in *The Vagabond* (Mutual, 1916); and slings his legs across Leo White's lap in *A Night Out* (Essanay, 1915)

Four examples of the Chaplin kick, front and back. From *Dough and Dynamite* (Keystone, 1914), both the front and the back kick, the back one especially, are delivered like ballet movements. The back kick to Ben Turpin's stomach occurs in *A Night Out* (Essanay, 1915). And the hefty kick to Mack Swain's bottom is in *Mabel's Married Life* (Keystone, 1914)

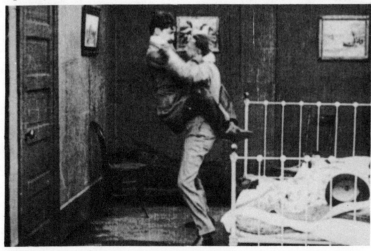

Charlie vaults into an irate husband's arms in *Making a Living* (Keystone, 1914) as a means of self-defence. This was a trick also used by Max Linder on many occasions

He is also true to the Commedia's tradition of lewdness. He feels the breasts of a tailor's dummy in *A Woman*, squirts a soda siphon at the genitals of a half-nude statue in *His New Job* and then touches them, and peers under the skirt of another nude statue in *Work*. *Twenty Minutes of Love* shows him sliding his hand up the thigh of a girl kissing her lover on a park bench, *A Night Out* gives him the chance to handle a woman's bottom in a hotel foyer and *The Count* finds him taking the strangest measurements of a girl who has come for a clothes fitting.

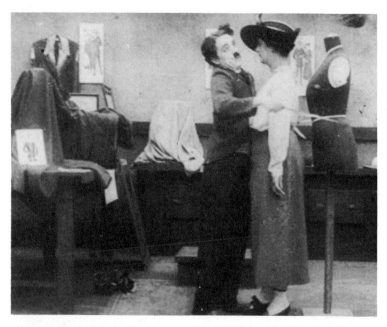

'...taking the strangest measurements
of a girl who has come for a clothes
fitting' in *The Count* (Mutual, 1916)

Tumbles and somersaults, the dangerous backward fall which he was capable of executing on a couple of stairs as in *The Rounders*, his famous skid-turn with one leg thrown out sideways like an admonishing index finger, the tricks with his hat, like making it jump by bending the brim and then letting it go, or like rolling it along his arm from shoulder to waist – all this was the stuff of the Commedia. But the resemblances do not stop there. The team that he gathered about him and which he always used so that they grew accustomed to his methods and temperament, the way his actors would contribute their own ideas or efface themselves from a scene so as to allow him to become the

'...his famous skid turn' in *The Count*
(Mutual, 1916)

focus of attention, the sketchy plots that only he seemed to know, the well-oiled routine that had taken half a day of working out on the set yet which still remained open to spontaneity – in short, the whole informal, intimate atmosphere surrounding the early Chaplin films – harked back to the days of the Commedia troupes, with their *lazzi*, their stock stories and their star actor-manager. Years later, after someone had drawn his attention to the Commedia's work, Chaplin was astonished to find how close it was to his own.

Early films, which Chaplin must have seen or perhaps heard about as a young boy, were also to play a part in his development. While making *Mabel at the Wheel* he tried to persuade Mabel Normand, who was directing, into allowing him to perform some business involving a water hose. He was to stand on it and thus cut off the water while closely inspecting the hose, only to step off and receive a jet of water full in the face. As early as 1896 the Lumière brothers projected in London a short diversion entitled *Teasing the Gardener* which anticipated Chaplin's suggestion in practically every detail. A naughty child steps on a garden hose and stops the water. A puzzled gardener peers down the nozzle, the child steps off and the gardener is drenched. In London in the same year Robert W. Paul made a film on the roof of the Alhambra theatre using a primitive set arranged to look like a park. It was called *The Soldier's Courtship*. A nusemaid and her soldier sweetheart are seated on a bench when an old lady arrives and sits next to them. Making a thorough nuisance of herself, she edges up to the young couple and forces them further and further along the bench. Suddenly they rise simultaneously and the old woman falls to the ground, bringing the bench down on top of her. In *Twenty Minutes of Love*, also set in a park, Chaplin arrives at a bench occupied by a kissing couple, and sits down. After simpering at them for a while he becomes bolder and drops his hand on to the girl's thigh, whereupon she changes places with her lover. Chaplin then begins to push him and, not unnaturally, the man pushes back. After several seconds of mutual retaliation, Chaplin suddenly stands and, caught by surprise, the man hurtles over the edge.

The park must have meant a great deal more to Chaplin than merely a convenient location, for he returned to it in *Recreation*, *His New Profession*, *Those Love Pangs*, *His Trysting Place* and *In the Park*. Perhaps he was partly determined in his choice by the fact that in the London that he knew the park represented the freedom he craved for, an immediate escape from the surrounding squalor. Periodically in Hollywood he was to feel the same compulsion to escape, and maybe these were the times when he felt the need to set his film in a park. But it also held sad memories for him. His autobiography carries a description of an outing spent with his mother in Kennington Park when she had taken a day off from the workhouse, and it is a curious fact that, with the exception of *His New Profession*, all his park films contain episodes of Chaplin failing to make contact with a woman, a symbolic representation of his relationship with his mother. *Those Love Pangs* is almost entirely devoted to his failings with women, *His Trysting Place* shows Mack Swain commiserating with him in a park after Chaplin has been thrown out by his wife. *In the Park* reveals Chaplin making unsuccessful attempts to flirt with a nursemaid, one of the characters in R. W. Paul's film; and *Recreation* begins with Chaplin preparing to drown himself in a park lake, in despair at his lack of female companionship.

Among other early films which Chaplin would have seen were those of André Deed, already mentioned as being known as 'Foolshead' in England, where he enjoyed a great vogue. He is likely to have exerted some influence on Chaplin and may well have supplied at least one of the 'Little Fellow's' characteristics. Deed, of course, explored many of the avenues leading to chaos, and his mindlessness was his

A foretaste of the pathos to come was given by Chaplin in one of the rare quieter moments of his Keystone period. As Chester Conklin makes off with a girl in *Those Love Pangs* (Keystone, 1914), Charlie's comic mask drops for a brief moment and the face registers genuine sadness

salient contribution to screen clowning. Though not as catastrophic in its results, the 'Little Fellow's' idiocy – as, for example, when he washes dishes in a tureen of soup in *Shanghaied*, or passes wet plates through a clothes drier in *The Pawnshop*, or breaks eggs with a hammer in *The Vagabond* – shows something of Deed's delight in the absurd. Nevertheless, Deed's humour was but a pale shadow of Chaplin's, and it was obviously Max Linder among French comedians who influenced Chaplin the most. Linder's great play with his hat and stick, his attention to tiny, humorous details, his somewhat seedy elegance and contempt for what he considered to be beneath him, find strong echoes in Chaplin's screen creation. The many visits that Chaplin was reported to have paid to Linder's films, both in Paris, when he was appearing in a Karno sketch, and in the United States, where he was known deliberately to seek them out, evince more than a passing interest.

After Linder, it is Mabel Normand who must rank as second in the list of those who contributed towards the success of the 'Little Fellow'.

MABEL NORMAND

Mabel Normand, one of the silent
screen's most popular and gifted
comediennes

The silent screen's finest comedienne, with a natural fluency of timing and a bubbling imagination, she was the first to recognize Chaplin's talent and to nurture its development. After *Mabel's Strange Predicament*, the first film in which he played opposite her, Chaplin showed a steady improvement in his style. After an exhaustive study of the films she made before Chaplin arrived on the scene, Samuel Peeples, a film historian, was forced to conclude that they contained 'entire routines, gestures, reactions, expressions, that were later a part of Chaplin's characterizations'.[7]

Normand, of course, was part of the Sennett stable, and the Keystone brand of comedy, though inimical to Chaplin in many ways, was also important to him in several others. Obviously it taught him the rudiments of film making, and Sennett himself is witness to the number of occasions Chaplin would remain behind at the studios when most of the others had left in order to work alongside the editor or to ask questions of any technician who happened to be there. Sennett, himself a product of the Biograph studios where D. W. Griffith reigned supreme, not only instructed Chaplin in how to achieve tension by cross-cutting between two concurrent events, but impressed upon him the need to shoot all exterior scenes in the open air and all interior scenes in the studio.

One of the results of Sennett's influence was *Shanghaied*. Chaplin made Essanay buy a schooner for his exterior scenes and for his climax blew it up outside Los Angeles harbour. But before the explosion, Chaplin introduces a fast-moving sequence that cuts between a lighted stick of dynamite in the hold and the crooked owner of the ship who, having discovered that his daughter is on board, is rushing to save her. Technique apart, Sennett's taste for burlesque, as well as his obsession with policemen, found a ready disciple in Chaplin. The moments of pure burlesque that he manages to inject into his pictures are really part of the 'Little Fellow's' character, as, for instance, his mimicry of the addictive gambler's type of routine in *His New Job* and *The Immigrant*, in which he performs a magnificent wind up of twists, shakes, rattles and muttered blessings before he throws the dice. For extended burlesque, however, one must look to *His Prehistoric Past* and *Carmen*. Both satirize current trends in film making. The first is based on a Griffith film – a rather ponderous one called *Man's Genesis* about a prehistoric age and a hero called 'Weakhands'. Chaplin plays him as 'Weakchin', and in spite of wearing a bearskin, still retains his bowler and cane. The second, *Carmen*, selects as its target the lavish production and adaptation of the novel that Jesse Lasky and De Mille brought out in 1915. Chaplin plays 'Darn Hosiery' to Edna Purviance's Carmen. The film has little to commend it except for a sword duel

*His Prehistoric Past* (Keystone, 1914) figured Charlie falling asleep on a park bench and dreaming of romance as a caveman. The device of a dream harked back to a sketch of his Karno days, and was to be employed again in *The Bank* (Essanay, 1915)

*Charlie Chaplin's Burlesque on Carmen* was expanded from two to four reels by Essanay after he had joined Mutual. They added a sub-plot featuring Ben Turpin. On its release in 1918, Chaplin sued them

'. . . in spite of wearing a bearskin still retains his bowler and cane'; *His Prehistoric Past* (Keystone, 1914)

'. . . with his sword held out like a fishing rod . . .'; *Charlie Chaplin's*

*Burlesque on Carmen* (Essanay, 1916)

between Chaplin and Escamille, in which a bored Darn Hosiery stands yawning with his sword held out like a fishing rod while his rival beats vainly against it.

This kind of ineptness is also shared by the policemen who appear from time to time. Aggressive they may be, but the 'Little Fellow' always gets the better of them. He spares them neither kicks nor blows, and *By The Sea* is a prime example of it. The film is one long fight from beginning to end, and in the midst of it all a policeman gets knocked out and Chaplin walks over his inert body.

Having therefore outlined the major influences at work on the 'Little Fellow', we can consider what is left, in the hope that by isolating it we have come part of the way in describing it.

Most people are agreed that one of Chaplin's finest sustained pieces of imaginative humour is the sequence in *The Pawnshop* when he examines the clock Albert Austin has brought in. Chaplin tests it with a stethoscope, taps it like a doctor, hits it with a hammer, drills it with a brace, opens the back with a can opener, inserts a telephone mouth-piece into his eye like a jeweller's glass and inspects the interior, pulls out the innards with a pair of pliers and, having cut up the spring into sections as if it were a piece of ribbon, sweeps up all the pieces into Austin's hat. The whole effect is one of an almost surrealistic treatment of objects. Things change their function or are placed in an alien context. Nevertheless, there is a kind of crazy logic running through it all, a perversenes in dealing with reality which, one senses, lies at the core of Chaplin's art. The humour itself, however, without Chaplin's little expressions and gestures, has its origins in an earlier age.

Grimaldi, the greatest of English clowns, who was at the height of his powers at the beginning of the nineteenth century, possessed just such an attitude towards the world of objects. He developed a majestic gift for mime and a disturbing way of employing it. His caricatures of a wide range of social types were exact and penetrating, but his imagination really caught fire when it created new associations between everyday things. The way he constructed a military dandy on stage, for example, was a marvel of ingenuity, and manifests the same style, timing and approach that went into Chaplin's virtuoso performance in *The Pawnshop*.

He would get a lady dressed in the height of fashion to cross the stage carrying an enormous muff. Joe would make love to her – no one could make love like Joe – he would steal the muff and stick it on his head. This would form the busby. A man enters selling brushes; he steals a pair, and wears one each side of his face. These form whiskers. Pantaloon borrows a pair of huge coal scuttles. These he (Grimaldi) puts on for boots. A carpenter crosses the stage,

MR. GRIMALDI AS — CLOWN IN MOTHER BUNCH.
As Performed at the Theatre Royal Covent Garden

Grimaldi in the make-up and costume
which was to influence all future
clowns

and Joey takes his saw from him for a sword. He steals a ring
knocker from the door of a house. This is the eye glass. Joe now struts
about the stage with the glass to his eye, saying 'Damme, sir!' after
the approved fashion of the modern Piccadilly dandy, and the
audience roar with laughter.[8]

An interesting paradox presented by both Grimaldi's and Chaplin's
technique is that while one assumes it to have sprung from an alert
and heightened consciousness, it could equally well be the result of a

'...waters the flowers on a hat'; *The Floorwalker* (Mutual, 1916)

numbed one. A drunkard who mistakes a street lamp for the moon has made the same imaginative leap. In *Caught in the Rain*, Chaplin tries to open his door with a cigarette instead of a key and pours whisky over his hair instead of hair oil; in *The Floorwalker* he treats the shop's cosmetic counter as his own bathroom and waters the flowers on a hat. The humour is identical, but in the first film he is drunk and in the second he is sober. In Chapter 3 we have already gone into the role drink played in the lives of the late Victorians, with its position in popular culture and its promise of release from a brutalizing environment. Chaplin was fascinated by it. As well as being brilliant at portraying drunkenness – he had become one of Karno's leading lights by his rendering of the 'Inebriated Swell' in *Mumming Birds* – it was also a subject he returned to again and again. The first film over which he had complete control pictures him as a drunk, and throughout his career the bottle was never far from the 'Little Fellow's' lips. Even in as late a film as *Limelight*, the first sight we catch of Chaplin is as he staggers home, obviously incapably drunk. Granted that the subject was a common one in the music hall, melodrama and the cinema, it would be wrong to suppose that that was the only reason why Chaplin was so drawn towards it. The idea of drunkenness, if not the fact of it, fulfilled a deep-seated need, for it allowed him to merge fantasy with reality. That this was fundamental to his character there can be little

Playing a drunk allowed Chaplin to indulge himself in his most characteristic behaviour: that of dealing arbitrarily with the inanimate world. In *The Rounders* (Keystone, 1914), he balances himself precariously along the straight border of the carpet. In *A Night Out* (Essanay, 1915), he brushes his teeth with the foliage around the hotel fountain and treats the telephone like a soda siphon. But it is in *One A.M.* (Mutual, 1916) that this attitude is taken to extremes.

Drunk throughout, he imagines himself under attack from practically every object in the house

doubt. His many and varied statements on his birth and childhood, the strange, dreamlike quality of much of his autobiography, are the expressions of a man for whom the dividing line between what is and what might be has always remained arbitrary.

The result is a comedy which is basically anarchic. It confuses categories, dislocates time, and tends to disorientate people. It can appear in a number of disguises. One can view it as plain idiocy: Chaplin trying to lift a stretcher while still standing on it in *The Adventurer*. It can be seen as absentmindedness: Chaplin scratching his

Beer becomes hair oil as well as foot
lotion in *The Champion* (Essanay, 1915)

hat instead of his head in *His New Job*. It is frequently brilliantly inventive: Chaplin treating the head on an animal rug as human and giving it a magnificent brush, shampoo and friction in *Behind the Screen*. Logic may be tortured by it: Chaplin as the caretaker in *The Bank*, finding it difficult to sweep up pieces of paper, picks them up, screws them into balls, replaces them carefully on the carpet, and only then sweeps them away. Often it throws our preconceptions out of

Charlie catches a fly by snatching it in mid-air, and then crushes it in his pocket – a nonsensical action carried out with superb naturalness in *The Vagabond* (Mutual, 1916)

gear: having gone through the complicated routine of opening a strong-room at the beginning of *The Bank*, Chaplin emerges with a mop and pail. (The same idea is reused in *The Pawnshop* when Chaplin takes out his sandwiches from a safe.) It can divert an anticipated or premeditated course of action, and thus can be successfully used against an opponent: arrested by a policeman in *The Adventurer*, Chaplin suddenly introduces Edna Purviance to his captor who automatically shakes hands with her and so allows Chaplin to escape.

'. . . arrested by a policeman in *The Adventurer*' (Mutual, 1917), 'Chaplin suddenly introduces Edna Purviance to his captor . . .' Frank J. Coleman is the luckless policeman

The list of examples could go on almost indefinitely, but it is already plain that they are linked together by a common theme. One might call it incongruity, the situation when two planes of reality not normally associated with each other are suddenly brought together. It is not surprising, therefore, that one of the many qualities ascribed to Chaplin's art is that it disturbs, for in a literal sense this is quite true. It disturbs arrangements of people or things, makes nonsense of cause and effect, reduces divisions to an absurdity. When he uses his cane like a billiard cue to pot a cake and then goes on to thrust it into a chicken like a sword, he is telling us that nothing need be what it seems. We laugh because we are released from the tension of being momentarily thrown off balance, but there is also something fascinating about a man who confronts us with a looking-glass world. The overthrow of order, the sudden inversion of all we take for granted, touches us deeply in our nature and liberates our imaginations.

This, then, was Chaplin's unique contribution to silent-film comedy. No other comedian exploited and used incongruity as he did. But at the same time it was a gift that created problems. The elusiveness of the 'Little Fellow's' character was almost wholly due to it. By itself, incongruity is neutral, it expresses nothing beyond the hypothesis

Lighting a cigarette with a pistol is
one way of reducing cause and effect
to an absurdity; *A Film Johnnie*
(Keystone, 1914)

that odd conjunctions of objects, people and ideas are funny. It makes
no comment upon the significance of those conjunctions. There need
be no sense of purpose behind them, no point of view. Incongruity
exists in its own right and, like an abstract painting, creates its own

'. . . and then goes on to thrust his cane into a chicken like a sword . . .'; *The Count* (Mutual, 1916). This film also contains the idea of the sight of something round sparking off an association with a game of billiards, Chaplin using his cane like a cue to hit fruit on a table. His next film, *The Pawnshop* (Mutual, 1916), contains the same joke

DELLUC, LOUIS, *Charlie Chaplin*, London: The Bodley Head, 1922
An appreciative and perceptive study of Chaplin's comic style by a leading French film director, playwright and journalist.

EASTMAN, MAX, *Enjoyment of Laughter*, London: Hamish Hamilton, 1937
A close friend assesses Chaplin's humour according to his own view of comedy.

FAURÉ, ELIE, *The Art of Cineplastics*, Boston: The Four Seas Co., 1923
A somewhat pretentious analysis of the psychological effects of Chaplin's costume and movements.

FLOREY, ROBERT, *Charlie Chaplin*, Paris: Jean Pascal, 1927
Chaplin's early career seen by a French film-maker who spent a lot of time in Hollywood. (In French.)

FOWLER, GENE, *Father Goose*, New York: Covici Friede, 1934
A biography of Mack Sennett which describes Chaplin's arrival at Keystone, his relationship with his fellow workers, the origins of his costume and the development of his acting style.

FRANK, WALDO DAVID, *Time Exposures*, New York: Boni & Liveright, 1926
Penetrating but subjective study of Chaplin's character.

FROHMAN, DANIEL, *Daniel Frohman Presents . . .* , New York: Claude Kendall & Willoughby Sharp, 1935
Anecdotes about Chaplin's pre-cinema career, with particular reference to his appearance in William Gillette's *Sherlock Holmes*.

GALLAGHER, J. P., *Fred Karno, Master of Mirth and Tears*, London: Robert Hale, 1971.
Another biography of the famous master of mirth who was so influential in Chaplin's early career.

GIFFORD, DENIS, *Chaplin*, London: Macmillan, 1974
A well-researched and well-documented but essentially lightweight account of Chaplin's career with good coverage of his pre-cinema life and a comprehensive bibliography and filmography.

GILLETTE, WILLIAM, *The Painful Predicament of Sherlock Holmes*, U.S.A.: privately printed by Ben Abramson, 1955.
Script of the one-act play in which Chaplin appeared as Billy at the Duke of York's Theatre, 1905.

GOLDWYN, SAUMEL, *Behind the Screen*, New York: George H. Doran, 1923
The discovery of Chaplin, his work for Sennett and relationship with Mabel Normand and the audience reaction to his films.

HANNON, WILLIAM MORGAN, *The Photodrama – Its Place Among the Fine Arts*, New Orleans: Ruskin Press, 1915
A serious analysis of Chaplin's early films.

HUFF, THEODORE, *Charlie Chaplin*, London: Cassell, 1952
Still the best all-round book on Chaplin and his films. Includes biographies of his fellow actors and associates.

JACOBS, LEWIS, *The Rise of the American Film*, New York: Harcourt Brace, 1939
A standard history of the American cinema which successfully places Chaplin's significance in perspective.

LAHUE, KALTON C., *Mack Sennett's Keystone*, London: Thomas Yoseloff, 1971
Chaplin's prolific output for Keystone seen in relation to the company's other films.

LAHUE, KALTON C., *The World of Laughter*, University of Oklahoma Press: Norman, 1966
A history of the film comedy from 1910–30.

LAWSON, JOHN HOWARD, *The Theory and Technique of Playwriting and Screenwriting*, New York: G. P. Putnam's Sons, 1949
Examines the structure of some of the Mutual films from a writer's standpoint.

LEJEUNE, C. A., *Cinema*, London: Maclehose, 1931
Contrasts Chaplin with Keaton, Lloyd and Langdon, and considers Chaplin's timing, balance and improvization.

MCCAFFREY, DONALD W., *Four Great Comedians: Chaplin, Lloyd, Keaton and Langdon*, London: Tantivy Press, 1968
A good study of Chaplin, the film-maker.

MCCAFFREY, DONALD W. (ed.), *Focus on Chaplin*, New Jersey: Prentice-Hall, 1971
An important collection of mainly contemporary articles on Chaplin's career, working methods and art.

MCDONALD, GERALD D., MICHAEL CONWAY and MARK RICCI, *The Films of Charlie Chaplin*, New York: Citadel, 1965
Synopses, contemporary reviews and a comprehensive collection of stills and frame enlargements.

MCDONALD, GERALD D., *The Picture History of Charlie Chaplin*, New York: Nostalgia Press, 1965
An odd but engaging collection of Chaplinana.

MANVELL, ROGER, *Chaplin*, London: Hutchinson, 1975
A workmanlike account of Chaplin's life from his early days in London to the present by Britain's most prolific writer on the cinema.

MELLOR, G. J., *The Northern Music Hall*, Newcastle-on-Tyne: Frank Graham, 1970
A well-researched account of the music hall in the North of England, including details of Chaplin's appearances.

MINNEY, R. J., *Chaplin: The Immortal Tramp*, London: George Newnes, 1954
An intimate in-depth study of Chaplin, the man and his films, by a friend.

MITRY, JEAN, *Tout Chaplin*, Paris: Éditions Seghers, 1972
Excellent synopses, credits, comment and background information on all Chaplin's films (in French).

MONTGOMERY, JOHN, *Comedy Films*, London: Allen & Unwin, 1954
Chaplin's films seen in relation to the work of other film comedians.

PAYNE, ROBERT, *The Great Charlie*, London: André Deutsch, 1952
A somewhat pretentious study of Chaplin's genesis and his influence on the cinema and the world.

POULAILLE, HENRY, *Charles Chaplin*, Paris: Bernard Grasset, 1927
Probably the best of the many biographies in French which cover Chaplin's early career.

QUIGLEY, ISABEL, *Charlie Chaplin: Early Comedies*, London: Studio Vista, 1968
A delightful and well-illustrated study of Chaplin's Keystone, Essanay and Mutual films.

RAMSAYE, TERRY, *A Million and One Nights*, 2 vols., New York: Simon & Schuster, 1926
Chaplin's early days at Keystone, his discovery of Edna Purviance and his financial negotiations.

REED, LANGFORD, *The Chronicles of Charlie Chaplin*, London: Cassell, 1917
Fictionalized versions of the Essanay films, including descriptive passages, intended to give the reader an idea of Chaplin's screen business and characterizations.

ROBINSON, CARLYLE T., *The Private Life of Charlie Chaplin*, New York: 1966
Chaplin seen by the man who was his secretary and factotum for sixteen years.

ROBINSON, DAVID, *The Great Funnies: A History of Film Comedy*, London: Studio Vista, 1969
A brief history of film comedy related in a concise and sympathetic way.

SAVIO, FRANCESCO (ed.), *Il Tutto Chaplin*, Venice Biennele dé Venezia: mostra internazionale d'arte cinematografica, 1972
Scripts of all his films issued in connection with the Chaplin retrospective at the Venice Film Festival in 1972 (in Italian).

SELDES, GILBERT, *An Hour with the Movies and the Talkies*, Philadelphia: Lippincott, 1929
Chaplin's unique capacity for seeing reality in terms of fantasy.

SELDES, GILBERT, *The Seven Lively Arts*, New York: Harper, 1924
Serious examination of the structure of Chaplin's early films and his capacity for tenderness and seriousness.

SENNETT, MACK and CAMERON SHIPP, *King of Comedy*, London: Peter Davies, 1955
An entertaining but impressionistic account of life on the Keystone lot.

TYLER, PARKER, *Chaplin: The Last of the Clowns*, New York: Vanguard Press, 1947
An idiosyncratic and sometimes pretentious analysis of Chaplin's artistry by an independent American film theorist.

TURCONI, DAVIDE, *Mack Sennett*, Rome: Edizioni del Anteneo, 1961
A well-researched book on Sennett by a leading Italian film historian.

VON ULM, GERITH, *Charlie Chaplin: King of Tragedy*, Idaho: Caxton Printers, 1940
A serious and perceptive biography.

WAGENKNECHT, EDWARD, *The Movies in the Age of Innocence*, Norman: University of Oklahoma Press, 1962
A delightful and captivating book about the early cinema as seen by an intelligent member of the audience.

# Filmography

The following filmography covers all the films in which Chaplin appeared that were produced during the Keystone, Essanay and Mutual periods (1914–17). Any new filmography must lean heavily on the work done by previous biographers. We owe particular thanks in this connection to Theodore Huff's *Charlie Chaplin*, Uno Asplund's *Chaplin's Films* and Denis Gifford's *Chaplin* (see Bibliography). Wherever it is known, we have included the English release date. This often varies from the American release date which appears in Huff or Gifford, and the Swedish release date quoted in Asplund.

## Keystone Period
All Keystone films were produced by Mack Sennett.

---

### MAKING A LIVING
US – 2 Feb. 14  GB – 18 Jun. 14  1,030 ft
*Reissue titles:* A Busted Johnny;
Troubles; Doing his Best; Take my
Picture
*Director:* Henry Lehrman
*Photography:* E. J. Vallejo
*Screenplay:* Reed Heustis
*Cast:* Chaplin (swindler), Henry
Lehrman (reporter), Virginia Kirtley
(his fiancée), Alice Davenport (her
mother), Chester Conklin
(policeman/tramp), Minta Durfee
(lady in the bedroom)

### KID AUTO RACES AT VENICE (CALIFORNIA)
US – 7 Feb. 14  GB – 2 Jul. 14  572 ft
*Reissue titles:* The Children's
Automobile Race; The Pest; A
Militant Suffragette
*Director:* Henry Lehrman
*Photography:* Frank D. Williams
*Screenplay:* Henry Lehrman
*Cast:* Chaplin (the tramp), Henry
Lehrman (the film director), Frank D.
Williams (the cameraman), Billy
Jacobs, Gordon Griffith, Thelma
Salter, Charlotte Fitzpatrick (the
children)

### MABEL'S STRANGE PREDICAMENT
US – 9 Feb. 14  GB – 22 Jun. 14  1,010 ft
*Reissue title:* Hotel Mix-up
*Directors:* Henry Lehrman and Mack
Sennett
*Photography:* Frank D. Williams
*Screenplay:* Reed Heustis
*Cast:* Chaplin (drunk), Mabel
Normand (elegant lady), Harry
McCoy (her admirer), Chester
Conklin (elderly man in room), Alice
Davenport (his wife), Al St John,
Hank Mann

### BETWEEN SHOWERS
US – 28 Feb. 14  GB – 9 Jul. 14  1,020 ft
*Reissue titles:* The Flirts; Charlie and
the Umbrella; In Wrong; Thunder
and Lightning
*Director:* Henry Lehrman
*Photography:* Frank D. Williams
*Screenplay:* Henry Lehrman
*Cast:* Chaplin (a young man), Ford
Sterling (friend and rival), Emma
Clifton (girl trying to cross street),
Chester Conklin (policeman), Sadie
Lampe (girl he flirts with)

### A FILM JOHNNIE
US – 2 Mar. 14  GB – 13 Jul. 14  1,020 ft
*Reissue titles:* Movie Nut; Million
Dollar Job
*Director:* George Nichols
*Photography:* Frank D. Williams
*Screenplay:* Craig Hutchinson
*Cast:* Chaplin (the 'johnnie'),
Virginia Kirtley (the Keystone girl),
'Fatty' Arbuckle (himself), Mabel
Normand (herself), Ford Sterling
(himself), Mack Sennett (himself),
Minta Durfee (an actress)

### TANGO TANGLES
US – 9 Mar. 14  GB – 10 Sep. 14  734 ft
*Reissue titles:* Charlie's Recreation;
Music Hall; A Tango Tangle
*Director:* Mack Sennett
*Photography:* Frank D. Williams
*Screenplay:* Mack Sennett
*Cast:* Chaplin (dandy), Ford Sterling
(band leader), 'Fatty' Arbuckle
(clarinettist), Minta Durfee
(cloakroom attendant), Chester
Conklin (dancer)

HIS FAVORITE PASTIME
US – 16 Mar. 14 GB – 20 Jul. 14
1,009 ft
*Reissue titles:* The Bonehead;
Charlie's Reckless Fling
*Director:* George Nichols
*Photography:* Frank D. Williams
*Screenplay:* Craig Hutchinson
*Cast:* Chaplin (drunk), 'Fatty'
Arbuckle (man at bar), Peggy Pearce
(lady in the taxi)

CRUEL, CRUEL LOVE
US – 26 Mar. 14 GB – 17 Sep. 14
1,035 ft
*Reissue title:* Lord Helpus
*Director:* George Nichols
*Photography:* Frank D. Williams
*Screenplay:* Craig Hutchinson
*Cast:* Chaplin (the lord), Minta
Durfee (the elegant young lady),
Alice Davenport (the maid), Chester
Conklin (the lord's butler)

THE STAR BOARDER
US – 4 Apr. 14 GB – 8 Oct. 14 1,020 ft
*Reissue titles:* The Hash-House Hero;
The Landlady's Pet; In Love with
His Landlady; The Fatal Lantern
*Director:* George Nichols
*Photography:* Frank D. Williams
*Screenplay:* Craig Hutchinson
*Cast:* Chaplin (a boarder), Minta
Durfee (his landlady), Alice
Davenport (the landlady's friend),
Edgar Kennedy (the landlord),
Gordon Griffith (the landlord's son)

MABEL AT THE WHEEL
US – 18 Apr. 14 GB – 17 May 15
1,900 ft
*Reissue titles:* A Hot Finish; His
Daredevil Queen
*Directors:* Mack Sennett and Mabel
Normand
*Photography:* Frank D. Williams
*Cast:* Chaplin (the saboteur), Harry
McCoy (the racing driver), Mabel

Normand (his girl friend), Chester
Conklin (her father), Mack Sennett
(reporter), Al St John, Fred Mace, Joe
Bordeaux, William Seiter (the
saboteur's henchmen)

TWENTY MINUTES OF LOVE
US – 20 Apr. 14 GB – 28 Sept. 14
1,009 ft
*Reissue titles:* The Love Fiend; Cops
and Watches; He Loved Her So
*Director:* Joseph Maddern
*Photography:* Frank D. Williams
*Screenplay:* Charles Chaplin
*Cast:* Chaplin (a vagabond), Minta
Durfee (the girl on the bench), Edgar
Kennedy (her boy friend), Emma
Clifton (second girl on bench),
Chester Conklin (her boy friend, the
thief), Joseph Swickard (his victim),
Gordon Griffith (a young boy)

CAUGHT IN A CABARET
US – 27 Apr. 14 GB – 9 Nov. 14
2,053 ft
*Reissue titles:* The Jazz Waiter;
Charlie the Waiter; Faking with
Society; The Waiter
*Directors:* Mabel Normand and
Charles Chaplin
*Photography:* Frank D. Williams
*Screenplay:* Charles Chaplin
*Cast:* Chaplin (a waiter), Mabel
Normand (a society girl), Harry
McCoy (her boy friend, the count),
Alice Davenport (her mother),
Joseph Swickard (her father), Edgar
Kennedy (the café proprietor), Minta
Durfee (a dancer), Chester Conklin
(another waiter), Mack Swain (the
thug), Gordon Griffith (a young boy),
Alice Howell, Wallace MacDonald
(customers and café staff)

## CAUGHT IN THE RAIN

US – 27 Apr. 14   GB – 21 Sep. 14
1,015 ft
*Reissue titles:* At It Again; Who Got
Stung; In the Park
*Director:* Charles Chaplin
*Photography:* Frank D. Williams
*Screenplay:* Charles Chaplin
*Cast:* Chaplin (a flirt), Alice
Davenport (the wife), Mack Swain
(the husband), Alice Howell (a girl)

## A BUSY DAY

US – 7 May 14   GB – 12 Nov. 14   441 ft
*Reissue titles:* Lady Charlie; A
Militant Suffragette; Busy As Can Be
*Director:* Charles Chaplin
*Photography:* Frank D. Williams
*Screenplay:* Charles Chaplin
*Cast:* Chaplin (a jealous wife), Mack
Swain (her husband), Alice
Davenport (his girl friend)

## THE FATAL MALLET

US – 1 Jun. 14   GB – 19 Nov. 14
1,120 ft
*Reissue titles:* The Pile Driver; Hit
Him Again; The Rival Suitors
*Directors:* Mack Sennett and Mabel
Normand
*Photography:* Frank D. Williams
*Screenplay:* Mack Sennett
*Cast:* Chaplin (the rival), Mabel
Normand (the girl), Mack Sennett
(her boy friend), Mack Swain
(another rival)

## HER FRIEND THE BANDIT

US – 4 Jun. 14   GB – 3 Dec. 14   993 ft
*Reissue titles:* Mabel's Flirtation; The
Thief Catcher
*Directors:* Mabel Normand and
Charles Chaplin
*Photography:* Frank D. Williams
*Cast:* Chaplin (the uninvited guest),
Mabel (the society lady), Charles
Murray (the Count de Beans)

## THE KNOCKOUT

US – 11 Jun. 14   GB – 10 May 14
1,960 ft
*Reissue titles:* Counted Out; The
Pugilist
*Director:* Charles Avery
*Photography:* Frank D. Williams
*Cast:* Chaplin (the referee), Edgar
Kennedy (Cyclone Flynn, the
champion), 'Fatty' Arbuckle (the
challenger), Minta Durfee (his girl
friend), Hank Mann (a boxer), Mack
Swain (an aggressive spectator),
'Slim' Summerville, Charley Chase,
Al St John, Mack Sennett, Alice
Howell (spectators), Edward Cline,
Joe Bordeaux (policemen)

## MABEL'S BUSY DAY

US – 13 Jun. 14   GB – 23 Nov. 14
998 ft
*Reissue titles:* Hot Dogs; Charlie and
the Sausages; Love and Lunch; Hot
Dog Charlie
*Directors:* Mabel Normand and
Charles Chaplin
*Photography:* Frank D. Williams
*Cast:* Chaplin (a swell), Mabel
Normand (girl who sells hot dogs),
Chester Conklin (policeman),
Edgar Kennedy, 'Slim' Summerville
(policemen), Billie Bennett (a girl),
Harry McCoy, Al St John, Charley
Chase, Wallace MacDonald

## MABEL'S MARRIED LIFE

US – 20 Jun. 14   GB – 30 Nov. 14
1,015 ft
*Reissue titles:* The Squarehead; When
You're Married
*Directors:* Mabel Normand and
Charles Chaplin
*Photography:* Frank D. Williams
*Cast:* Chaplin (the ineffectual
husband), Mabel Normand (his
wife), Hank Mann (a friend), Alice
Davenport (a neighbour), Mack
Swain (Mr Wellington, the lady-

killer), Alice Howell (his wife),
Charles Murray, Harry McCoy (men
at the bar), Al St John, Wallace
MacDonald (delivery men)

## LAUGHING GAS

US – 9 Jul. 14  GB – 4 Jan. 15  1,020 ft
*Reissue titles:* Tuning His Ivories;
The Dentist; Down and Out; The
Busy Little Dentist
*Director:* Charles Chaplin
*Photography:* Frank D. Williams
*Screenplay:* Charles Chaplin
*Cast:* Chaplin (the dentist's assistant),
Fritz Schade (Dr Pain, the dentist),
Alice Howell (his wife), Joseph
Swickard, 'Slim' Summerville
(patients), Mack Swain (a passer-by),
Joseph Sutherland (the dentist's other
assistant)

## THE PROPERTY MAN

US – 1 Aug. 14  GB – 29 Mar. 15
2,118 ft
*Reissue titles:* Getting His Goat; The
Roustabout; Props; Charlie on the
Boards; The Vamping Venus
*Director:* Charles Chaplin
*Photography:* Frank D. Williams
*Screenplay:* Charles Chaplin.
*Cast:* Chaplin (the property man),
Fritz Schade (Garlico, the weight-
lifter), Phyllis Allen (Hamlena Fat),
Alice Davenport, Norma Nichols
(vaudeville artistes), Mack Sennett
(man in the audience in pullover),
Charles Bennett, Joe Bordeaux
(actors), Harry McCoy, Lee Morris

## THE FACE ON THE BAR-ROOM FLOOR

US – 10 Aug. 14  GB – 4 Feb. 15
1,002 ft
*Reissue titles:* The Ham Artist; The
Ham Actor
*Director:* Charles Chaplin
*Photography:* Frank D. Williams
*Screenplay:* Charles Chaplin (from a

poem by Hugh Antoine D'Arcy)
*Cast:* Chaplin (the artist), Cecile
Arnold (Madeleine), Fritz Schade
(wealthy client who marries
Madeleine), Vivian Edwards (a
model), Chester Conklin, Hank
Mann, Harry McCoy, Wallace
MacDonald (drinkers)

## RECREATION

US – 13 Aug. 14  GB – 25 Feb. 15
462 ft
*Reissue title:* Spring Fever
*Director:* Charles Chaplin
*Photography:* Frank D. Williams
*Screenplay:* Charles Chaplin
*Cast:* Chaplin (man walking in the
park), Charlie Murray (the seaman),
Norma Nichols (his girl friend)

## THE MASQUERADER

US – 27 Aug. 14  GB – 1 Mar. 15
1,030 ft
*Reissue titles:* Putting One Over;
The Female Impersonator; The
Perfumed Lady; The Picnic; His
New Profession (erroneously)
*Director:* Charles Chaplin
*Photography:* Frank D. Williams
*Screenplay:* Charles Chaplin
*Cast:* Chaplin (actor/beautiful lady),
'Fatty' Arbuckle (actor), Chester
Conklin, Fritz Schade, Charley Chase,
Harry McCoy (actors), Charles
Murray (film director), Minta Durfee
(the heroine), Cecile Arnold, Vivian
Edwards (actresses)

## HIS NEW PROFESSION

US – 31 Aug. 14  GB – 8 Mar. 15
1,015 ft
*Reissue titles:* The Good for Nothing;
Helping Himself
*Director:* Charles Chaplin
*Photography:* Frank D. Williams
*Screenplay:* Charles Chaplin
*Cast:* Chaplin (the male nurse),
Charley Chase (young man with

invalid uncle), Norma Nichols (his girl friend), Fritz Schade (the invalid uncle), Cecile Arnold (young man's second girl friend), Harry McCoy (policeman)

## THE ROUNDERS
US – 5 Sep. 14 GB – 25 Mar. 15
1,010 ft
*Reissue titles:* Revelry; Two of a Kind; Oh What a Night; Going Down; The Love Thief; Tip Tap Toe
*Director:* Charles Chaplin
*Photography:* Frank D. Williams
*Screenplay:* Charles Chaplin
*Cast:* Chaplin (Mr Full), Phyllis Allen (his wife), 'Fatty' Arbuckle (Mr Fuller), Minta Durfee (his wife), Fritz Schade, Charley Chase, Wallace MacDonald (diners), Al St John (bellhop)

## THE NEW JANITOR
US – 24 Sep. 14 GB – 11 Mar. 15
1,020 ft
*Reissue titles:* The Porter; The New Porter; The Blundering Boob
*Director:* Charles Chaplin
*Photography:* Frank D. Williams
*Screenplay:* Charles Chaplin
*Cast:* Chaplin (the janitor), Fritz Schade (his boss), Minta Durfee (secretary), Jack Dillon (the thief), Al St John (lift boy)

## THOSE LOVE PANGS
US – 10 Oct. 14 GB – 15 Mar. 15
1,010 ft
*Reissue titles:* The Rival Mashers; Busted Hearts; Oh You Girls
*Director:* Charles Chaplin
*Photography:* Frank D. Williams
*Screenplay:* Charles Chaplin
*Cast:* Chaplin (young man), Vivian Edwards (the girl he falls for in the park), Edgar Kennedy (her stupid friend), Chester Conklin (his rival),

Cecile Arnold (the girl he falls for in the park), Norma Nichols (the landlady), Harry McCoy (the policeman)

## DOUGH AND DYNAMITE
US – 26 Oct. 14 GB – May 1916
2,010 ft
*Reissue titles:* The Doughnut Designer; The Cook
*Directors:* Charles Chaplin and Mack Sennett
*Photography:* Frank D. Williams
*Screenplay:* Charles Chaplin
*Cast:* Chaplin (Pierre, waiter-cum-baker), Chester Conklin (Jacques, the waiter-cum-baker), Fritz Schade (M. La Vie, owner of the restaurant), Cecile Arnold, Vivian Edwards (waitresses), Charley Chase, 'Slim' Summerville, Wallace MacDonald, Edgar Kennedy (bakers), Norma Nichols (Madame La Vie, the proprietor's wife), Phyllis Allen, Jack Dillon (customers)

## GENTLEMEN OF NERVE
US – 29 Oct. 14 GB – 5 Jul. 15 1,030 ft
*Reissue titles:* Some Nerve; Charlie at the Races
*Director:* Charles Chaplin
*Photography:* Frank D. Williams
*Screenplay:* Charles Chaplin
*Cast:* Chaplin (Mr Wow-Wow, man who enters race-track through fence), Mack Swain (Ambrose, his friend), Chester Conklin (Walrus), Mabel Normand (his girl friend), Phyllis Allen (his wife), Edgar Kennedy (a policeman), Charley Chase, 'Slim' Summerville (spectators), Alice Davenport (a waitress)

## HIS MUSICAL CAREER

us – 7 Nov. 14  GB – 20 May 15
1,025 ft
*Reissue titles:* The Piano Movers;
Musical Tramps
*Director:* Charles Chaplin
*Photography:* Frank D. Williams
*Screenplay:* Charles Chaplin
*Cast:* Chaplin (Tom, the removal
man), Mack Swain (Ambrose,
another removal man), Fritz Schade
(Mr Rich, a wealthy customer),
Alice Howell (Mrs Rich, his wife),
Charley Chase (manager of the music
shop), Joe Bordeaux (Mr Poor, the
seedy artist), Norma Nichols (Mrs
Poor, his wife)

## HIS TRYSTING PLACE

us – 9 Nov. 14  GB – unknown
1,912 ft
*Reissue titles:* Family House; The
Ladies' Man; The Henpecked
Spouse; Very Much Married
*Director:* Charles Chaplin
*Photography:* Frank D. Williams
*Screenplay:* Charles Chaplin
*Cast:* Chaplin (Clarence, the inept
husband), Mabel Normand (Mabel,
his wife), Mack Swain (Ambrose),
Phyllis Allen (his wife)

## TILLIE'S PUNCTURED
## ROMANCE

us – 14 Nov. 14  GB – May 1916
4,796 ft
*Reissue titles:* Marie's Millions; For
the Love of Tillie; Tillie's Big
Romance; Tillie's Nightmare
*Director:* Mark Sennett
*Photography:* Frank D. Williams
*Screenplay:* Hampton Del Ruth
(from Edgar Smith's play, *Tillie's
Nightmare*)
*Cast:* Chaplin (the professional lover),
Mabel Normand (Mabel, his
girl friend), Marie Dressler (Tillie, a
farmer's daughter), Mack Swain

(John Banks, her father), Charles
Bennett (Douglas Banks, Tillie's
uncle, the millionaire), Charley
Chase, Charles Murray (detectives),
Chester Conklin (Mr Whoozie, a
friend of Douglas Banks), Edgar
Kennedy (the restaurant owner),
Harry McCoy (pianist), Minta
Durfee (maid), Phyllis Allen
(waitress), Alice Davenport, Alice
Howell (guests), 'Slim' Summerville,
Al St John, Joe Bordeaux, Wallace
MacDonald, Hank Mann, Edward
Sutherland, G. G. Ligon (policemen),
Gordon Griffith (newsboy), Billie
Bennett (a girl), Rev. D. Simpson
(himself)

## GETTING ACQUAINTED

us – 5 Dec. 14  GB – 3 Jun. 15  1,025 ft
*Reissue titles:* A Fair Exchange; Hello
Everybody; Exchange is no Robbery
*Director:* Charles Chaplin
*Photography:* Frank D. Williams
*Screenplay:* Charles Chaplin
*Cast:* Chaplin (Mr Sniffles), Phyllis
Allen (his wife), Mack Swain (Mr
Ambrose), Mabel Normand (Mrs
Ambrose) Edgar Kennedy (a
policeman) Harry McCoy (a Turk),
Cecile Arnold (a girl)

## HIS PREHISTORIC PAST

us – 7 Dec. 14  GB – unknown
1,945 ft
*Reissue titles:* A Dream; King Charlie;
The Caveman; The Hula-Hula Dance
*Director:* Charles Chaplin
*Photography:* Frank D. Williams
*Screenplay:* Charles Chaplin
*Cast:* Chaplin (Mr Weakchin), Mack
Swain (King Lowbrow), Gene Marsh
(Sum-Babee, his favourite wife),
Fritz Schade (Ku-ku, the king's
medicine man), Cecile Arnold (a
cavewoman), Al St John (a caveman)

Essanay Period
All Essanay films were produced by Jesse J. Robbins.

HIS NEW JOB
US – 1 Feb. 15  GB – 20 May 15
1,996 ft
*Reissue title:* Charlie's New Job
*Director:* Charles Chaplin
*Photography:* 'Rollie' Totheroh
*Screenplay:* Charles Chaplin
*Cast:* Chaplin (a film extra), Ben
Turpin (a film extra), Charlotte
Mineau (the star), Charles Insley
(the film director), Leo White
(actor, the hussar officer), Frank J.
Coleman (assistant director), Bud
Jamison (the star who arrives late),
Billy Armstrong, Agnes Ayres,
Gloria Swanson (extras)

A NIGHT OUT
US – 10 Feb. 15  GB – 3 Jun. 15  1,961 ft
*Reissue titles:* Charlie's Night Out;
Charlie's Drunken Daze; Champagne
Charlie; His Night Out
*Director:* Charles Chaplin
*Assistant director:* Ernest van Pelt
*Photography:* 'Rollie' Totheroh and
Harry Ensign
*Screenplay:* Charles Chaplin
*Cast:* Chaplin (a drunk), Ben Turpin
(a drunk), Leo White (a French
customer in the restaurant), Bud
Jamison (the head waiter), Edna
Purviance (his wife), Fred Goodwins
(diner)

THE CHAMPION
US – 5 Mar. 15  GB – 17 Jun. 15
1,939 ft
*Reissue titles:* Champion Charlie;
Battling Charlie; Charlie the
Champion
*Director:* Charles Chaplin
*Assistant director:* Ernest van Pelt
*Photography:* 'Rollie' Totheroh and
Harry Ensign
*Screenplay:* Charles Chaplin

*Cast:* Chaplin (tramp/challenger),
Bud Jamison (the champion), Lloyd
Bacon (the trainer), Edna Purviance
(his daughter), Leo White (the crook),
Carl Stockdale, Billy Armstrong,
Paddy McGuire (sparring partners),
Ben Turpin (salesman in a beret),
'Broncho' Billy Anderson
(enthusiastic spectator)

IN THE PARK
US – 12 Mar. 15  GB – 1 Jul. 15
984 ft
*Reissue titles:* Charlie on the Spree;
Charlie in the Park
*Director:* Charles Chaplin
*Assistant director:* Ernest van Pelt
*Photography:* 'Rollie' Totheroh and
Harry Ensign
*Screenplay:* Charles Chaplin
*Cast:* Chaplin (man walking in the
park), Edna Purviance (a nursemaid),
Bud Jamison (her boy friend),
Leo White, Margie Reiger (the
lovers), Billy Armstrong (hot-dog
man), Lloyd Bank (the thief), Ernest
van Pelt (policeman)

THE JITNEY ELOPEMENT
US – 23 Mar. 15  GB – 15 Jul. 15
1,968 ft
*Reissue title:* Married in Haste;
Charlie's Elopement
*Director:* Charles Chaplin
*Assistant director:* Ernest van Pelt
*Photography:* 'Rollie' Totheroh and
Harry Ensign
*Screenplay:* Charles Chaplin
*Cast:* Chaplin (the tramp), Edna
Purviance (the girl he is in love with),
Fred Goodwins (her father), Leo
White (the Count de Ha-Ha), Paddy
McGuire (the old retainer), Lloyd
Bacon (the footman), Carl Stockdale,
Ernest van Pelt, Bud Jamison
(policemen)

## THE TRAMP
US – 7 May 15   GB – 22 Jul. 15   1,896 ft
*Reissue titles:* Charlie the Tramp;
Charlie on the Farm; Charlie the
Hobo
*Director:* Charles Chaplin
*Assistant director:* Ernest van Pelt
*Photography:* 'Rollie' Totheroh and
Harry Ensign
*Screenplay:* Charles Chaplin
*Cast:* Chaplin (the tramp), Fred
Goodwins (the farmer), Edna
Purviance (his daughter), Lloyd
Bacon (her boy friend), Paddy
McGuire (a farmhand), Leo White,
Bud Jamison, Ernest van Pelt (the
thieves), Billy Armstrong (a poet)

## BY THE SEA
US – 26 Apr. 15   GB – 12 Aug. 15
971 ft
*Reissue titles:* Charlie's Day Out;
Charlie by the Sea
*Director:* Charles Chaplin
*Assistant director:* Ernest van Pelt
*Photography:* 'Rollie' Tolheroh and
Harry Ensign
*Screenplay:* Charles Chaplin
*Cast:* Chaplin (man on the beach),
Billy Armstrong (the holidaymaker),
Margie Reiger (his girl friend), Edna
Purviance (the young wife), Bud
Jamison (her husband), Carl
Stockdale (the policeman)

## HIS REGENERATION
US – 3 May 15   GB – 30 Aug. 15   963 ft
*Producer:* 'Broncho' Billy Anderson
*Cast:* 'Broncho' Billy Anderson, Lee
Willard, Marguerite Clayton, Hazel
Applegate, Charles Chaplin

## WORK
US – 2 Apr. 15   GB – 1 May 16
2,017 ft
*Reissue titles:* The Paperhanger;
Charlie at Work; Charlie the
Decorator; Only a Working Man;
The Plumber

*Director:* Charles Chaplin
*Assistant director:* Ernest van Pelt
*Photography:* 'Rollie' Totheroh and
Harry Ensign
*Screenplay:* Charles Chaplin
*Scenic artist:* E. T. Mazy
*Cast:* Chaplin (the decorator's
assistant), Charles Insley (the
decorator), Edna Purviance (the
maid), Billy Armstrong (the
house-owner), Marta Golden (his
wife), Leo White (her lover), Paddy
McGuire (the hod carrier)

## A WOMAN
US – 7 Jul. 15   GB – 7 Oct. 15   1,785 ft
*Reissue titles:* The Perfect Lady;
Charlie, the Perfect Lady
*Director:* Charles Chaplin
*Assistant director:* Ernest van Pelt
*Photography:* 'Rollie' Totheroh and
Harry Ensign
*Screenplay:* Charles Chaplin
*Scenic artist:* E. T. Mazy
*Cast:* Chaplin (the gentleman who
poses as a woman), Charles Insley (the
father), Marta Golden (his wife),
Edna Purviance (their daughter),
Margie Reiger (the father's girl
friend), Billy Armstrong (the suitor),
Leo White (man in the park)

## THE BANK
US – 9 Aug. 15   GB – 28 Oct. 15
1,985 ft
*Reissue titles:* Charlie at the Bank;
Charlie in the Bank; Charlie,
Detective
*Director:* Charles Chaplin
*Assistant director:* Ernest van Pelt
*Photography:* 'Rollie' Totheroh and
Harry Ensign
*Screenplay:* Charles Chaplin
*Scenic artist:* E. T. Mazy
*Cast:* Chaplin (the bank janitor),
Edna Purviance (the secretary),
Charles Insley (the bank manager),
Carl Stockdale (Charlie, the cashier),

Billy Armstrong (another janitor), Leo White (a customer), Fred Goodwins (the doorman), Bud Jamison (customer/leader of gang of crooks), Wesley Ruggles, Frank J. Coleman, Paddy McGuire (the crooks), John Rand (a salesman), Carrie Clarke Ward

## SHANGHAIED
US – 27 Sep. 15 GB – 18 Nov. 15
1,771 ft
*Reissue titles:* Charlie the Sailor; Charlie on the Ocean; Charlie Shanghaied
*Director:* Charles Chaplin
*Assistant director:* Ernest van Pelt
*Photography:* 'Rollie' Totheroh and Harry Ensign
*Screenplay:* Charles Chaplin
*Scenic artist:* E. T. Mazy
*Cast:* Chaplin (a tramp), Edna Purviance (the ship-owner's daughter), Wesley Ruggles (the ship-owner), John Rand (the captain), Bud Jamison (the first mate), Leo White, Paddy McGuire, Fred Goodwins (shanghaied seamen), Billy Armstrong (the ship's cook), Lawrence A. Bowles (his assistant)

## A NIGHT IN THE SHOW
US – 2 Nov. 15 GB – unknown
1,735 ft
*Reissue title:* Charlie at the Show
*Director:* Charles Chaplin
*Assistant director:* Ernest van Pelt
*Photography:* 'Rollie' Totheroh and Harry Ensign
*Screenplay:* Charles Chaplin
*Scenic artist:* E. T. Mazy
*Cast:* Chaplin (Mr Pest, the man in the stalls/Mr Rowdy, the drunk in the circle), Edna Purviance (girl sitting next to Mr Pest), Leo White (Mr Nix, the conjuror/man in stalls/ man in box), Charlotte Mineau (Edna's neighbour in the stalls), John

Rand (conductor), Bud Jamison (Dot), James T. Kelley (Dash), Dee Lampton (fat boy in the box), May White (La Belle Winerwurst, the snake charmer/the fat lady who falls in the fountain), Paddy McGuire (trombonist), Fred Goodwins (tuba player), Wesley Ruggles (man in the gallery), Bud Jamison (the singer/ Edna's husband in the stalls), Phyllis Allen, Charles Insley (members of the audience), Carrie Clarke Ward (woman in box)

## CHARLIE CHAPLIN'S BURLESQUE ON CARMEN
US – 3 Apr. 16 GB – Jul. 1916 3,986 ft
*Reissue title:* Carmen
*Director:* Charles Chaplin
*Assistant director:* Ernest van Pelt
*Photography:* 'Rollie' Totheroh
*Screenplay:* Charles Chaplin (based on the story by Prosper Mérimée and the opera by Georges Bizet)
*Scenic artist:* E. T. Mazy
*Cast:* Chaplin (Darn Hosiery), Edna Purviance (Carmen), Ben Turpin (Don Remendado, a smuggler), Leo White (Morales, an officer of the guard), John Rand (Escamillo, the toredor), Jack Henderson (Lilias Pasta, the leader of the smugglers), May White (Frasquita), Bud Jamison (soldier), Wesley Ruggles (a tramp), Lawrence A. Bowles, Frank J. Coleman

## POLICE
US – 27 Mar. 16 GB – 11 Dec. 16
2,050 ft
*Reissue titles:* Charlie the Burglar; Charlie in the Police; The Housebreaker
*Director:* Charles Chaplin
*Assistant director:* Ernest van Pelt
*Photography:* 'Rollie' Totheroh
*Screenplay:* Charles Chaplin (from a story by Charles Chaplin and Vincent

Bryan)
*Scenic artist:* E. T. Mazy
*Cast:* Chaplin (Convict 999), Wesley
Ruggles (the thief), Edna Purviance
(the girl whose house is broken into),
Billy Armstrong (crook), James T.
Kelley (drunk who has pockets
picked/tramp), Leo White (fruitseller/
lodging-house keeper/policeman),
Fred Goodwins (bogus preacher/
policeman), John Rand, Frank J.
Coleman (policemen)

## TRIPLE TROUBLE
US – 23 Jul. 18  GB – 23 Jan. 19  1,460 ft
*Reissue title:* Charlie's Triple Trouble
*Directors:* Charles Chaplin and Leo
White
*Assistant director:* Ernest van Pelt
*Photography:* 'Rollie' Totheroh
*Screenplay:* Charles Chaplin and Leo
White
*Cast:* Chaplin (a kitchen boy), Edna
Purviance (the maid), Billy
Armstrong (crook/thief), Leo White
(a spy), James T. Kelley (singer),
Bud Jamison (a tramp), Wesley
Ruggles (a crook), Albert Austin (a
man)

The Mutual Period
All films produced by Charles Chaplin.

---

THE FLOOR WALKER
US – 15 May 16  GB – 23 Oct. 16
1,734 ft
*Reissue title:* Shop !
*Director:* Charles Chaplin
*Photography:* William C. Foster and
'Rollie' Totheroh
*Screenplay:* Charles Chaplin
*Scenic artist:* E. T. Mazy
*Cast:* Chaplin (the floorwalker), Eric
Campbell (the manager), Lloyd
Bacon (his assistant), Edna Purviance
(secretary), Albert Austin (shop
assistant), Lee White (French
customer), Charlotte Mineaū
(detective), Tom Nelson (detective),
Henry Bergman (old man), James T.
Kelley (lift boy)

THE FIREMAN
US – 12 Jun. 16  GB – 27 Nov. 16
1,921 ft
*Reissue titles:* A Gallant Fireman; The
Fiery Circle
*Director:* Charles Chaplin
*Photography:* William C. Foster and
'Rollie' Totheroh
*Story:* Charles Chaplin and Vincent
Bryan
*Screenplay:* Charles Chaplin
*Scenic artist:* E. T. Mazy
*Cast:* Chaplin (fireman), Edna
Purviance (the girl), Eric Campbell
(captain of fire brigade), Leo White
(man whose house burns down),
John Rand, Albert Austin, James T.
Kelley, Frank J. Coleman (firemen),
Charlotte Mineau (mother)

THE VAGABOND
US – 10 Jul. 16  GB – 23 Apr. 17
1,956 ft
*Reissue title:* Gypsy Life
*Director:* Charles Chaplin
*Photography:* William C. Foster and
'Rollie' Totheroh
*Story:* Charles Chaplin and Vincent
Bryan
*Screenplay:* Charles Chaplin
*Cast:* Chaplin (the vagabond
violinist), Edna Purviance (waif),
Eric Campbell (gypsy leader), Leo
White (old gypsy woman/old Jew),
Lloyd Bacon (young artist), Charlotte
Mineau (Edna's mother), Albert
Austin (trombonist), John Rand
(trumpeter), James T. Kelley, Frank
J. Coleman (musicians and gypsies),
Phyllis Allen (woman)

ONE A.M.
US – 7 Aug. 16  GB – 26 Mar. 17
2,034 ft
*Reissue title:* Solo
*Director:* Charles Chaplin
*Photography:* William C. Foster and
'Rollie' Totheroh
*Story/screenplay:* Charles Chaplin
*Scenic artist:* E. T. Mazy
*Cast:* Chaplin (the drunk), Albert
Austin (taxi driver)

THE COUNT
US – 4 Sep. 16  GB – 1 Jan. 17  2,017 ft
*Reissue title:* Almost a Gentleman
*Director:* Charles Chaplin
*Photography:* 'Rollie' Totheroh and
William C. Foster
*Story/screenplay:* Charles Chaplin
*Cast:* Chaplin (tailor's assistant), Eric
Campbell (Buttinsky, the tailor),
Edna Purviance (Miss Moneybags),
Charlotte Mineau (Mrs Moneybags),
Leo White (Count Broke), James T.
Kelley (butler), Frank J. Coleman
(policeman/guest), Eva Thatcher
(cook), Albert Austin, John Rand,
Stanley Sanford (guests), Leota
Bryan (girl), Loyal Underwood
(little old man)

## THE PAWNSHOP

US – 2 Oct. 16  GB – 18 Jan. 17  1,940 ft
*Reissue titles:* High and Low Finance;
At the Sign of the Dollar
*Director:* Charles Chaplin
*Photography:* 'Rollie' Totheroh and
William C. Foster
*Story/screenplay:* Charles Chaplin
*Cast:* Chaplin (pawnbroker's
assistant), Henry Bergman
(pawnbroker), Edna Purviance (his
daughter), John Rand (other
assistant), Eric Campbell (burglar),
Albert Austin, Wesley Ruggles,
James T. Kelley (customers),
Frank J. Coleman (policeman)

## BEHIND THE SCREEN

US – 13 Nov. 16  GB – 26 Feb. 17
1,796 ft
*Reissue titles:* The Pride of
Hollywood; Los Fallen Angeles
*Director:* Charles Chaplin
*Photography:* 'Rollie' Totheroh and
William C. Foster
*Story/screenplay:* Charles Chaplin
*Cast:* Chaplin (stagehand in film
studios), Edna Purviance (girl looking
for work in films), Eric Campbell
(stagehands' foreman), Henry
Bergman (director), Charlotte
Mineau, Leota Bryan (actresses),
Albert Austin, John Rand, Leo White
(stagehands), Wesley Ruggles, Tom
Wood (actors), Frank J. Coleman
(assistant director)

## THE RINK

US – 4 Dec. 16  GB – 21 May 17
1,881 ft
*Reissue titles:* Rolling Around;
Waiter!
*Director:* Charles Chaplin
*Photography:* 'Rollie' Totheroh and
William C. Foster
*Story/screenplay:* Charles Chaplin
*Cast:* Chaplin (waiter), Edna
Purviance (Miss Loneleigh, society

girl), Eric Campbell (Mr Stout),
Henry Bergman (Mrs Stout), James
T. Kelley (Edna's father), Albert
Austin (cook), John Rand (waiter),
Lloyd Bacon (customer), Frank J.
Coleman (manager of restaurant),
Charlotte Mineau, Leota Bryan
(friends of Edna)

## EASY STREET

US – 22 Jan. 17  GB – 18 Jun. 17
1,757 ft
*Director:* Charles Chaplin
*Photography:* 'Rollie' Totheroh and
William C. Foster
*Story/screenplay:* Charles Chaplin
*Cast:* Chaplin (vagabond), Edna
Purviance (girl working in Church
Mission), Henry Campbell
(neighbourhood tyrant), Albert
Austin (minister/policeman), Henry
Bergman (anarchist), Lloyd
Underwood (policeman/father),
Leota Bryan (mother), Tom Wood
(Chief of Police), Frank J. Coleman,
Leo White (policemen), Lloyd Bacon
(drug addict), Charlotte Mineau
(wife), James T. Kelley (missioner/
policeman), Janet Miller Sully, John
Rand (people in Mission)

## THE CURE

US – 16 Apr. 17  GB – 19 Jun. 16
1,834 ft
*Reissue title:* The Water Cure
*Director:* Charles Chaplin
*Photography:* 'Rollie' Totheroh and
William C. Foster
*Story/screenplay:* Charles Chaplin
*Cast:* Chaplin (drunk), Edna
Purviance (girl), Eric Campbell
(gout-ridden patient), Henry Bergman
(masseur), John Rand (attendant/
second masseur), Albert Austin
(attendant), James T. Kelley (bearded
bellhop), Frank J. Coleman (spa
director), Leota Bryan (nurse), Tom

Wood, Janet Miller Sully, Loyal
Underwood (patients)

## THE IMMIGRANT
US – 17 Jun. 17   GB – 9 Aug. 17
1,809 ft
*Reissue titles:* The New World; A
Modern Columbus; Hello U.S.A.
*Director:* Charles Chaplin
*Photography:* 'Rollie' Totheroh and
William C. Foster
*Story/screenplay:* Charles Chaplin
*Cast:* Chaplin (the Immigrant), Edna
Purviance (immigrant), Kitty
Bradbury (her mother), Albert
Austin (bearded immigrant/diner),
Henry Bergman (woman on boat/
artist), Eric Campbell (head waiter),
Stanley Sanford (gambler), James T.
Kelley (tramp/immigrant), John
Rand (guest), Frank J. Coleman
(proprietor/ship's officer), Loyal
Underwood (immigrant)

## THE ADVENTURER
US – 23 Oct. 17   GB – 17 Jan. 18
1,845 ft
*Director:* Charles Chaplin
*Photography:* 'Rollie' Totheroh and
William C. Foster
*Story/screenplay:* Charles Chaplin
*Cast:* Chaplin (escaped convict),
Edna Purviance (wealthy girl), Henry
Bergman (her father/workman),
Marta Golden (her mother), Albert
Austin (butler), Frank J. Coleman
(prison guard), James T. Kelley (old
man), Phyllis Allen (governess),
May White (lady), Kono (chauffeur),
John Rand (guest), Janet Miller Sully
(girl), Monta Bell (man)

# Index

(Italic figures indicate an illustration)

language. Meanings and qualities may be attributed to it, and indeed frequently are, which were not intended by its practitioner. There is no proof at all that when Chaplin wipes his eyes with a preacher's beard in *Police*, or shares a hymn-book with a baby in *Easy Street*, that he is making a comment on organized religion. It is much more likely that the subject was chosen, especially the mission hall in *Easy Street*, because it reminded him of his childhood and because it was a popular subject on the music-hall stage. The point is that the conditioning of his early years in London and in the theatre predisposed him towards certain subjects, but within that framework anything and everything could act as fuel for his imagination. A combination of any two objects, functions, ideas and actions, provided that their juxtaposition was incongruous, was all that he needed. Brilliant and amusing as they are, they state only that fantasy and reality are interchangeable. A child sits in an old, wooden box and it becomes a Rolls-Royce; faced with a large family of children, Chaplin feeds them like chickens. The

'. . . faced with a large family of children, Chaplin feeds them like chickens'; *Easy Street* (Mutual, 1917)

mechanism at work is the same and Chaplin is making no further comment than the child. And in this lies the 'Little Fellow's' elusiveness. If everything can be treated in the same way, if children can become chickens, a safe become a larder, a walking-stick a billiard cue and a bald head a mere surface on which to strike a match, how can we judge what is his own reality, his own point of view? The answer must be that we cannot, and that the more we pursue it, the more elusive it becomes.

## 10. References

1. Hal Roach in *Silent Picture*, Spring 1970.
2. R. J. Minney, *Chaplin, the Immortal Tramp*, London: Newnes, 1954.
3. J. P. Gallagher, *Fred Karno, Master of Mirth and Tears*, London: Robert Hale, 1971.
4. Max Beerbohm, 'The Humour of the Public', in *Yet More*, London: Heinemann, 1922.
5. ibid.
6. *Film Culture*, Spring 1972.
7. *Classic Film Collector*, Spring 1970; also in Denis Gifford, *The Movie Makers – Chaplin*, London: Macmillan, 1974.
8. *The Era*, March 1896.

# Bibliography

This select bibliography does not include all the books on Chaplin in foreign languages. A more complete list can be found in Denis Gifford's *Chaplin* (see below). Neither does it include articles on Chaplin or his films. Most articles in English which were published before 1940 can be found in the FILM INDEX – Vol. I: *The Film as Art* New York: The Museum of Modern Art Film Library and the H. H. Wilson Company, 1941. Later articles will probably be referred to in the books on this reading list.

Wherever applicable, the British publisher and publication date are given. However, many of the books were also published under different titles in other languages or in the United States. There have also been numerous reprints, reissues and paperback editions. More detailed information can be obtained from the British Film Institute Book Library, or through your local public library.

ADELER, EDWIN and CON WEST, *Remember Fred Karno?*, London: John Long, 1939
A biography of the man who taught Chaplin the art of mime.
ASPLUND, UNO, *Chaplin's Films*, London: Arts Book Society, 1973
Contains the most detailed synopses of Chaplin's films published in English, and a fascinating table of footages, running times and release dates gleaned from the annals of the Swedish Board of Censors.
BARRY, IRIS, *Let's Go to the Pictures*, London: Chatto & Windus, 1926
A study of the comedian as the Everyman of the twentieth century. Traces the evolution of his talent from *Making a Living* (1914) to *The Gold Rush* (1925).
BOWMAN, WM DODGSON, *Charlie Chaplin, his life and art*, London: Routledge, 1931
Chaplin's early life in Britain, his music-hall career and his first films, with an analysis of his characterization and his humour.
BROWNLOW, KEVIN, *The Parade's Gone By . . .*, London: Secker & Warburg, 1968
A compulsive and affectionate study of the American silent cinema, its directors and its stars.
BURKE, THOMAS, *City of Encounters*, London: Constable, 1932
A penetrating study of Chaplin's erratic creative processes by a novelist and life-long friend who experienced the same social origins.
CHAPLIN, CHARLIE, *Charlie Chaplin's Own Story*, Indianapolis: Bobbs-Merrill, 1916.
An ostensibly faithful account of Chaplin's career from his boyhood in London to the signing of his Mutual contract. A rare book because it was withdrawn immediately after publication at Chaplin's request. Copies are in the Library of Congress and the Swedish Film Institute Library. Sections are reprinted in Donald W. McCaffrey (ed.), *Focus on Chaplin* (see below).
CHAPLIN, CHARLIE, *My Wonderful Visit*, London: Hurst & Blackett, 1922
First-person narrative of his triumphant tour through Europe in 1921. Mainly a self-indulgent catalogue of the people he met.
CHAPLIN, CHARLES, *My Autobiography*, London: The Bodley Head, 1964
Chaplin's own story as he remembered it in his old age. Significant for its unintentional revelations and its omissions.
CHAPLIN, CHARLES, *My Life in Pictures*, London: The Bodley Head, 1974
A fine collection of photographs and frame enlargements covering the period from his childhood in Victorian London to the receipt of his Academy Award in 1971.
CHAPLIN, CHARLES, Jnr, N. RAU and M. RAU, *My Father, Charlie Chaplin*, New York: Random House, 1960
Chaplin's son sympathetically recalls life with father.
CODD, ELSIE, *Charlie Chaplin's Methods*, London: Standard Art Book Co., 1920
An account of Chaplin's working methods by his secretary, issued as lesson two in the series *Cinema: Practical Course in Acting*. Section reproduced in Donald W. McCaffrey (ed.), *Focus on Chaplin* (see below).
COTES, PETER and THELMA NIKLAUS, *The Little Fellow*, London: Paul Elek, 1951
A light but accessible account of Chaplin's career.

# Photographic Credits

The authors would like to thank all those film companies past and present who own the films illustrated. In particular: United Artists for illustrations from *The Gold Rush*, *The Circus* and *Modern Times* and Pathé for those from *Les Enfants du Paradis*.

Frame enlargements appear on the following pages: 37, 43, 44 (top), 56, 57, 77, 78, 88, 90, 91, 94, 98, 103, 107, 111, 113, 115 (top), 116, 118 (bottom), 121, 122, 123, 124, 125, 133, 134, 135 (centre & bottom), 140, 141, 145, 148, 161, 162, 163, 164, 165, 167, 168, 169, 170, 171, 172, 173 (left), 174, 176, 182, 183, 186, 187, 188, 189 (top & centre), 190 (top), 192 (top), 193 (top & centre), 194, 195 (top), 197, 198, 199, 201, 202 (except bottom right), 203, 204, 205, 207, 210, 213, 214, 215, 216, 217, 218, 219, 220 (top), 221.

Other illustrations are reproduced by courtesy of the following: Bradford City Library, page 67; Cinema Bookshop, pages 64, 68, 79, 89, 101 (top), 115 (bottom), 200, 202 (bottom right), 214 (bottom); Crown, page 62; Ellis Ashton Collection, pages 31, 53, 54, 71, 69, 70, 71, 125 (bottom right), 135 (top); *Les Grands Films Classiques*, pages 93 (bottom), 144 (bottom right), 196; John Huntley, page 143 (bottom); Samuel McKechnie, *Popular Entertainment through the Ages* (Sampson, Low, London), pages 185, 192 (bottom); National Film Archive, pages 11, 14, 15, 16, 17, 25, 30, 33, 34, 73, 87, 97, 99, 102, 118 (top), 129, 131, 132, 144 (top), 166, 175, 181 (bottom), 189 (bottom), 190 (bottom), 193 (bottom), 195 (bottom), 208, 210 (bottom), 220 (bottom); Theatre Museum, pages 109, 110, 114 (top), 117, 212; Authors' collection, pages 19, 20, 28, 29, 35, 36, 41, 42, 44 (bottom), 47, 49, 51, 52, 63, 93 (top), 100, 105, 106, 108, 114 (bottom), 125 (bottom left), 130, 142, 143 (top), 144 (bottom left), 153, 154, 160, 181 (top).